·REMEMBERING, WE FORGET·

REMEMBERING, WE · FORGET

A · BACKGROUND · STUDY · TO · THE POETRY · OF · THE
FIRST · WORLD · WAR

Hilda D Spear

·DAVIS · POYNTER · LONDON·

First published in 1979 by
Davis-Poynter Limited
20 Garrick Street London WC2E 9BJ

ISBN 0 7067 0235 2

The publisher acknowledges the financial assistance of the British Academy
and of the Carnegie Trust for the Universities of Scotland in the publication
of this volume.

Printed in Great Britain by
Robert MacLehose & Co. Ltd
Printers to the University of Glasgow

Remembering, we forget
Much that was monstrous, much that clogged our souls with clay
When hours were guides who led us by the longest way—
And when the worst had been endured could still disclose
Another worst to thwart us
Siegfried Sassoon
(from 'To One Who was With Me in the War')

·

TO
WALTER
GILLIAN
AND
KATHRYN

·

Limited for extracts from *Collected Poems* by Sir Herbert Read; to the Author's Estate and to Secker and Warburg Limited for extracts from *The Contrary Experience* by Sir Herbert Read; to Mr. G. T. Sassoon for extracts from work by Siegfried Sassoon; to the estate of Sir Osbert Sitwell and Duckworth for extracts from *Argonaut and Juggernaut* by Sir Osbert Sitwell; to the estate of Sir Osbert Sitwell and Macmillans for 'Ill-Winds' from *Noble Essences*; to Mr. M. B. Yeats, Miss Anne Yeats and the Macmillan Company of London and Basingstoke for extracts from *Collected Poems* by W. B. Yeats and from *The Variorum Edition of the Poems of W. B. Yeats*.

·CONTENTS·

· Acknowledgements ·

I SHOULD LIKE to acknowledge the encouragement and financial assistance given me by the British Academy and by the Carnegie Trust for the Universities of Scotland. I should also like to acknowledge the assistance of the Teachers' Research Fund of the University of Dundee.

Thanks are due for the help and encouragement given to me at various stages in my work by Mr. George Fraser; by Professor Clive Hart; by Professor Ivor Batchelor, with whom I had several interesting discussions on the psychiatric aspects of this study; by the late Mr. Harold Owen for information about his brother, Wilfred Owen, and for a useful correspondence over several years; by Mr. Patric Dickinson and Professor Joseph Cohen for their interest, especially in the early stages of this work; by the late Sir Osbert Sitwell and Mrs. Anne Tibble for lending me books; by the staff of Dundee University Library; and by Mrs. Elizabeth Burgon Barriss, Miss M. Blyth, Professor Harold Brooks, the Reverend Alexander Caseby, Mr. James Craigie, Mr. Roland Hall, Mrs. E. Rough and a multitude of others, too numerous to mention, especially people living in and around Dundee, who willingly answered my questions, lent me material and gave me information.

My special thanks and gratitude are due to Mrs. Moira Anthony who patiently typed and re-typed sections of this book and to my daughter Kathryn who has given me valuable assistance in proof-reading.

· Prefatory Note ·

THIS STUDY is concerned with the changing attitudes to war as they were manifested in contemporary writings, both personal and public, during the years 1914 to 1918; it attempts to demonstrate not only how the poetry of the period was a true reflection of men's thoughts and feelings, but also how it finally crystallized the new awareness to war which developed in that era.

In such a study a large number of references are necessary. I have tried, however, to keep notes to a minimum by giving as much information as possible in the text. The 'Notes' should be used in conjunction with the Bibliography in which details of all books referred to may be found. Where only one book by a particular author is listed all references to and quotations from his work refer to that book unless otherwise specified. For other authors the text or the notes specify the book used except in the case of a number of major authors to whom there are frequent references; for these, the Bibliography indicates the text used for all quotations and references unless otherwise specified.

Source of epigraphs for each chapter may be found in the Notes.

Hilda D. Spear
Dundee, June 1978

14

·INTRODUCTORY·

✦✦✦✦✦✦✦

> The lamps are going out all over Europe; we shall not
> see them lit again in our lifetime.

THE SPARK which set off the First World War was the murder at
Sarajevo on the 28th of June 1914 of the Archduke Franz Ferdinand,
heir to the Habsburg throne. It did not appear likely that a world
war would ensue. A. J. P. Taylor asserts that on the 5th of July
(upon which date he believes the decisions were made which led to
war), 'general war seemed hypothetical and remote.'[1] Certainly
Austria-Hungary was not swiftly aroused; its ultimatum to Serbia
was not presented until the 23rd of July, almost a month after the
Archduke's assassination. When Serbia rejected the ultimatum events
moved swiftly and surely to bring most of Europe into a conflict
which they scarcely understood. On the 28th of July Austria-Hungary
declared war on Serbia; on the 1st of August Germany followed suit
and two days later made general war inevitable by declaring war
against France. The British declaration followed on the 4th of
August.

*　　　　*　　　　*

When war came, it came to a Britain totally unprepared, except for
its navy, for warfare against a powerful enemy. It came too, to a
Britain surprised to find itself in conflict with a foreign enemy, for
matters much nearer home had been the grave concern of politicians
and newspapers for months past: during the vital days before war
was declared the question of Home Rule for Ireland was darkening
England with the threat of civil war. It was not until the 27th of July

15

that *The Times* devoted its first leader to international rather than internal affairs. But there was still no conviction of the inevitability of war:

> Should there arise in any quarter a desire to test our adhesion to the principles that inform our friendships and that guarantee the balance of power in Europe, we shall be found no less ready and determined to vindicate them with the whole strength of the Empire, as we have been found whenever they have been tried in the past. That, we conceive, interest, duty, and honour all demand from us. England will not hesitate to answer to their call.

The following day, the very day on which Austria-Hungary declared war, there was even less conviction, and *The Times'* first leader began with the reassuring words, 'The European situation is perceptibly less threatening than it was yesterday, although it still remains very anxious and insecure'. The truth was that the nation had been lulled into a sense of security with regard to international war. Writing of the pre-war Cabinet, A. J. P. Taylor declared that 'they did not believe that England could be endangered by events on the Continent.'[2]

By the beginning of August the British public had at last become aware of the possibility of war. On the 3rd of August *The Times* reported Bank holiday crowds eagerly buying up the latest editions of the morning papers and instantly becoming 'engrossed in the news from abroad'. Their reaction to this sudden revelation of impending war was natural. Events in far-away Serbia seemed to have little relation to Britain and British interests. The *Daily News* for the same day announced:

> There is no war party in this country. On the contrary, the horrors of war have already seized on the popular imagination, and in the highways and public vehicles in London yesterday, the populace were heard to express their indignation at the swift and tragic movements on the Continent.

This pacific mood was merely transient. While Britain was outside the war it was remote from the hearts of the British people, for most of whom Serbia and Sarajevo were no more than names. The threats to neighbouring France and to 'little Belgium', however, were swiftly realized, and the proclamation of war on the 4th of August brought with it a change of attitude that was overwhelming. The next day *The Times* reported that the crowds which gathered to hear the Proclamation of War read were 'filled with the war spirit', and the *Daily News* which two days earlier had affirmed that 'there is no war party in this country', now described how the 'enthusiasm culminated outside Buckingham Palace when it became known that war had been declared'. Newspapers and periodicals of the first month of the war did much to encourage the wave of fervent patriotism and war-eagerness which swept over the country, and it was not long before every available wall bore the famous poster of Kitchener with its pointing finger and arresting caption, 'Your King and Country Need You'. On the 12th of August *The Times* was able to report that young men were queueing all day outside the Central Recruiting Office at Great Scotland Yard in response to Kitchener's call for 100,000 men: 'The work of enlistment proceeded briskly all day, and new recruits were sworn in at the rate of between 80 and 100 an hour'.

There was scarcely a discordant voice anywhere in the country. Internal strife and party faction were forgotten. The fighting spirit of Ireland was diverted from civil to world war, and divisions of Irishmen were soon ready to join in the greater conflict. Amidst all this enthusiasm it is sobering to read a letter from Lord Weardale in *The Times* for the 5th of August. This letter shows him to have been one of the most clear-sighted statesmen Britain could boast of in those troublous days. He seemed to have sure premonitions of the horrors to come and the day after war was declared he wrote,

The indignation of Austria at the crime of Sarajevo is as natural as the racial and religious sympathy of Russia with the Servian people; but what rational man can contend that such a question and such temporary antagonisms can justify the horrors of a great European war—the worst, perhaps, the world has ever seen—with its countless dead and maimed, its ruined homes, its irremediable industrial losses? Both victors and vanquished can only emerge from such a conflict bankrupt in resources and in all the higher attributes of humanity.

His was the voice in the wilderness proclaiming the true and deadly character of the war. Before long he would be joined by others who spoke not from a lively apprehension of what war could mean, but from the terrible experience of twentieth-century warfare.

Meanwhile the war was on and enlistment continued, and among those who enlisted during the next few years were the young men who were to become the voice and the conscience of their age—the poets of England: Edmund Blunden, Rupert Brooke, Robert Graves, Wilfred Owen, Isaac Rosenberg, Siegfried Sassoon, to mention only some of the better known. When war broke out Siegfried Sassoon, who was the oldest of these young men, was twenty-eight; Edmund Blunden was seventeen. Even the most sensitive scarcely foresaw the horrors that were before them. Although Wilfred Owen wrote in 1914:

> *War broke: and now the Winter of the world*
> *With perishing great darkness closes in*[3]

he yet wrote home in a letter to his mother on New Year's Day 1917 when he first joined the fighting forces in France: 'There is a fine heroic feeling about being in France, and I am in perfect spirits. A tinge of excitement is about me'.

It was mainly this 'tinge of excitement' which prevailed during the first two years of war. In his journal for August 1914 Aubrey Herbert wrote, 'The men were very pleased to have been under fire, and compared notes as to how they felt',[4] but the Battle of Mons in which his men were then engaged was followed by the Battle of Le Cateau and of the Marne and the first Battle of Ypres. Meanwhile Antwerp had fallen and the hopes of peace 'before Christmas' began to recede. The tone of reports from the Front began to change: on the 28th of August 1914 *The Times* reported from the Battle of Mons that the British soldier 'was cheerful, steady and confident'; six weeks later, on the 8th of October, another report told how the wounded were 'as happy and as eager to be well enough to go to the front again as if they were schoolboys going home for the holidays'. But a sourer note was creeping into the reports: first, the confession that war and the idea of war were two very different things; many men began to realize that their notions of war had been false, like the officer who wrote to *The Times* for the 4th of December 1914, 'I had not the slightest conception what war could mean, even in the wildest flights of fancy'; secondly, there were descriptions of the real horrors of war, such as this, again from an officer's letter to *The Times*, but several months later, on the 5th of April 1915, 'You cannot imagine what a battlefield is like after a battle—a huddled mass of corpses, some of which have been lying there since the fighting here in October last'; and thirdly, there were the beginnings of condemnation:

By the touchstone of the men it has broken this war is judged and the makers of this war. And more than ruined villages and desecrated churches these soldiers pronounce condemnation. They, who have given so much, are, in a sense, without joy and without enthusiasm; rather they shun recollection. There is no zest in the killing of men. . . . The war is revealed as a thing gross and dull-witted, a crime even against the ancient, chivalrous spirit of war.[5]

During 1915 the frontiers of war were extended and its horrors intensified. Early in the year Zeppelin raids were made on England; in February the Germans began their U-boat blockade of Britain; and in April, on the Western Front, during the second battle of Ypres, the Germans launched their first gas attack. The allied offensives which followed were largely indecisive and by the end of the year the enthusiasm of 1914 was beginning to wane. In a letter to his mother two days after Christmas, Alan Seeger wrote of 'the immense secret longing for peace that is the universal undercurrent in Europe now'.

Despite the loss of American lives from German U-boat attacks, the United States had so far avoided any sort of commitment in the war. In January 1916, however, President Wilson made his first peace move; it was done secretly by sending his adviser, Colonel House, to Europe to negotiate. The attempt was entirely unsuccessful and was not renewed until the end of the year, by which time the Germans had stolen the initiative from the Americans and made their own peace offer. Yet in 1916, politically, Europe was not ready for peace. However, it was in that year that the heart seemed to go out of the men fighting the war.

To begin with, the Military Service Act of January 1916 sent to France men who were not volunteers, but conscripts, men who had not chosen but rather were being compelled to fight. Secondly, the troubles in Ireland which had dissolved themselves in the greater European troubles at the beginning of the war surged up again with the Easter Rising. The violence with which this was put down and the harshness of the punishments meted out to the rebels caused an unrest and dissatisfaction which the British government had hardly expected. Thirdly, the Battle of the Somme, which began on the 1st of July and dragged on until mid-November, stands as a classic example of the foolishness and futility of war. The command on both sides committed errors and sacrificed lives without understanding and without sympathy. Over a million British, French and German soldiers gave their lives to achieve nothing, or very little. Those who were left began to realize the true nature of the war. As A. J. P. Taylor states,

> Idealism perished on the Somme. The enthusiastic volunteers were enthusiastic no longer. They had lost faith in their cause, in their leaders, in everything except loyalty to their fighting comrades. The war ceased to have a purpose. It went on for its own sake, as a contest in endurance.[6]

The year petered out. Both the German and the American Peace moves were rejected. After the peace negotiations had failed war seemed more hopeless and less right. Men had ceased to believe any longer in the cause they were fighting for; this resulted in feelings of guilt that they were the instruments by which the war was being prolonged; they had, as Sir Herbert Read put it, 'no moral sanction to support the spirit'.[7]

At last, in April 1917, the U.S.A. declared war on Germany. It seemed to make little difference: the war of attrition dragged on. New peace proposals were put forward by Germany in July and by the Pope in August but to the politicians on both sides the final acceptable solution had not been found. Whilst the proposals were being discussed the third battle of Ypres was being fought; 'Passchendaele' as it was known was the most terrible battle of the war, and

> all the combatants engaged on either side regarded it as the culmination of horror. . . . The rain was pitiless, the ubiquitous mud speedily engulfed man and beast if a step was taken astray from the narrow duckboards, upon which descended a perpetual storm of shells and gas.[8]

In November, with the reports of the casualties and horrors of Ypres still coming in, Lord Lansdowne made an attempt to bring about a compromise peace. In a letter published in the *Daily Telegraph* on the 29th of November he insisted that,

> We are not going to lose this war, but its prolongation will spell ruin for the civilized world. . . . What will be the value of the blessings of peace to nations so exhausted that they can scarcely stretch out an arm with which to grasp them?

Lord Lansdowne's plea for peace and the *Daily Telegraph's* publication of it were supported by the *Daily News* and the *Manchester*

Guardian but *The Times* opposed them. The war dragged on.

It was Philip Gibbs's reporting of the third battle of Ypres that moved Lloyd George to write to C. P. Scott in December:

> I warn you, I am in a very pacifist temper. I listened last night to Philip Gibbs on his return from the Front, to the most impressive and moving description from him of what the war in the West really means, that I have heard. . . . If people really knew, the war would be stopped tomorrow, but of course they don't know—and can't know. . . . The thing is horrible and beyond human nature to bear, and I feel I can't go any longer with the bloody business; I would rather resign.[9]

But, of course, he did not resign and the war dragged on.

The spring of 1918 saw repeated offensives by the Germans along the Western front and then gradually the tide began to turn. By early October the Germans were suing for peace and negotiations drifted on until the Armistice was finally signed on the 11th of November.

In four and a quarter years of war about 13,000,000 men had been killed and almost 20,000,000 wounded.

*   *   *

> *When you see millions of the mouthless dead*
> *Across your dreams in pale battalions go,*
> *Say not soft things as other men have said,*
> *That you'll remember. For you need not so.*
> *Give them not praise. For, deaf, how should they know*
> *It is not curses heaped on each gashed head?*
> *Nor tears. Their blind eyes see not your tears flow.*
> *Nor honour. It is easy to be dead.*[10]

·CHAPTER·ONE·

Who is the happy Warrior? Who is he
That every man in arms should wish to be?

TWO WORLD WARS, and times of peace which have been nothing if not precarious, separate our generation from the men of 1914. During the last sixty years there has been no time, politically speaking, when we have been able to feel secure, for our background has been constantly one of war and world turmoil. Today we cannot imagine the advent of war being greeted with rapture. But the background to the lives of the men who went to war in 1914 was one of peace and they had at first no language nor aura of thought by which they could describe their new experience.

It was perhaps inevitable, therefore, that the romantic attitude should be the first to sweep through the country since in 1914 no other attitude had been clearly formulated. Literature had fostered the romance, for in general even the most realistic accounts had shown war to be not without honour. The poets had spoken of battle and death but the conventional approach had been to describe them in terms of glory and patriotism. The poems which Sir Henry Newbolt was publishing round about the turn of the century and during the years preceding the war, illustrate this point very well. In an era of peace he looked back to such battles as Trafalgar, which represented for him the greatness of England, and in which he saw nothing but courage and nobility:

> *Lover of England, stand awhile and gaze*
> *With thankful heart, and lips refrained from praise;*
> *They rest beyond the speech of human pride*
> *Who served with Nelson and with Nelson died.*[1]

23

As an older poet (he was fifty-two years old when war broke out) his message to youth extolled the martial virtues: the public school spirit was one which should endure through adult life:

> *To set the cause above renown*
> *To love the game beyond the prize,*
> *To honour, while you strike him down,*
> *The foe that comes with fearless eyes.*[2]

When war broke out, men's first impulses were towards its romance, for academically, in 1914 war *was* romantic. This romanticism was apparent in various attitudes to war, all of them completely unrelated to the essence of war itself, none of them embodying a philosophy able to stand up to the realities of actual battle, yet in themselves real enough to express a large part of what war meant to a peaceful generation. And what war meant to most men at that time was something personal and individual; when they enlisted they did not consider the wider implications of war; their action was essentially thoughtless and essentially selfish. 'Getting out to the Front', wrote Siegfried Sassoon, 'had been an ambition rather than an obligation.'[3] Had it been otherwise, romanticism would have died with the war's inception, for it is only in sheer egoism that the romance of war thrives. It is not surprising that men turned to poetry to express their sudden upsurge of emotions, for the act of writing poetry has in itself a romantic aura. For many it was a sentimental exercise, lacking even an ephemeral truth, but of the innumerable poems written in the early days of the war some at least reflected the true spirit of the times.

A simple, yet not necessarily naïve, classification can be made by suggesting that the writer of true romantic war poetry was writing for and of himself, whereas the writer of sentimental poetry was writing for and of others; the romantic writer was generally a participant, wanting something personal from war and something which only war seemed able to give—glory, honour, freedom, escape; he may have been mistaken, but he was at least sincere; he did not reflect every facet of his life in war, but he reflected certain facets which at a particular moment of time appeared to him to be important. The sentimental writer, on the other hand, was generally a non-combatant, writing without personal involvement, seeing war impersonally as glorious and honourable. The romantic participant often used exaggerated vocabulary but he rarely sentimentalized. He would not

24

write a poem such as that by Robert Vernède published in *The Times* for the 19th of August 1914:

> *Lad, with the merry smile and the eyes*
> > *Quick as a hawk's and clear as the day,*
> *You, who have counted the game the prize,*
> > *Here is the game of games to play,*
> *Never a goal—the captains say—*
> > *Matches the one that's needed now:*
> *Put the old blazer and cap away—*
> > *England's colours await your brow.*

Notice the falsifying of standards, the equating of war with a game and of the soldiers' uniform with the school colours, the exploitation of men's finer feelings by the captain's appeal, the evocation of the clean young Englishman in the first two lines and the sentimental use of the word 'lad'. It is propaganda, written not from the heart but from the head.

But compare Vernède's lines with (say) the second and best of Rupert Brooke's sonnet sequence:

> *War knows no power. Safe shall be my going,*
> > *Secretly armed against all death's endeavour;*
> *Safe though all safety's lost; safe where men fall;*
> *And if these poor limbs die, safest of all.*[4]

Here the poet is writing of himself; we may feel that his view of war is mistaken but he is not offering it as a game; in these concluding four lines he faces up to the possibility of death in war—his own and that of others—and embraces it, not through any lack of sincerity, but because death would capture for ever a particular moment of time.

The insidiousness of such sentimentality as that of Vernède's poem was that it touched a chord in men's minds and won a false response from them. As Donald Hankey explained:

When war broke out the public school man applied for his commission in the firm conviction that war was a glorified form of big-game hunting— the highest form of sport. His whole training, the traditions of his kind, had prepared him for that hour. From his earliest schooldays he had been taught that it was the mark of a gentleman to welcome danger, and to regard the risk of death as the most piquant sauce to life.[5]

In a letter to his father written on the 8th of August 1916 Lt. H. P. M. Jones took up for himself Vernède's metaphor of the football game: 'in my heart and soul I have always longed for the rough-and-tumble of war as for a football match.'[6] Yet, like Vernède when he wrote his poem, Jones had not at that time really experienced war; though he was in France, he was still merely an observer, waiting to become a participant. It is ironic to find that by this time Vernède, now fighting in France, was writing home to his wife in a very different vein: 'I suppose I have just found out what [war] can be like. . . . I still think it's right that [it] should be damnable, but I wish everybody could have an idea of how beastly it can be'.[7]

Such complete turnabouts make it difficult to understand that the romantic attitude was indeed very real, and also to distinguish between what was frankly sentimental with false values and false emotions and what stemmed from more genuine and more personal feelings. Fair judgment is particularly difficult when one considers poetry written during the war by older poets such as Thomas Hardy. At the outbreak of war Hardy was seventy-four years old. His poetic gift had matured late in life and because of this he was poetically very aware. 'Men Who March Away', written on the 5th of September 1914 chimes well with the spirit of the time:

> *What of the faith and fire within us*
> > *Men who march away*
> > *Ere the barn-cocks say*
> > *Night is growing gray,*
> *Leaving all that here can win us;*
> *What of the faith and fire within us*
> > *Men who march away?*

> *   *   *

> *In our heart of hearts believing*
> > *Victory crowns the just,*
> > *And that braggarts must*
> > *Surely bite the dust,*
> *Press we to the field ungrieving,*
> *In our heart of hearts believing*
> > *Victory crowns the just.*

> *Hence the faith and fire within us*
> > *Men who march away.*[8]

During the years of war, however, he became increasingly unable to identify spiritually with the war generation. In his very balanced chapter on Hardy in *Out Of Battle* Jon Silkin writes of 'his seemingly distorted response'. Such distortion is perhaps not surprising: an old man, a non-combatant, Hardy was aligned with authority, with the non-combatants, rather than with the soldiers, the victims, as can be seen from 'A Call to National Service' written in March 1917:

> *Up and be doing, all who have a hand*
> *To lift, a back to bend.*

>   *   *   *

> *—Say, then, 'I come!' and go, O women and men . . .*
> *That scareless, scathless, England still may stand.*

> *Would years but let me stir as once I stirred*
> *At many a dawn to take the forward track,*
> *And with a stride plunged on to enterprize,*

> *I now would speed like yesterwind that whirred*
> *Through yielding pines; and serve with never a slack,*
> *So loud for promptness all around outcries!*

His failure to progress in thought from ideas of courage, honour and patriotism indicates his lack of spiritual involvement with the experiences of the later war years. This is perhaps made more, rather than less obvious by his poem written 'On the signing of the Armistice, November 11th, 1918'. Its title 'And there was a Great Calm' is taken from the New Testament account of Christ stilling the waves, an idea in itself oddly out of accord both with the tone of the poem and with the time, for Christ had 'rebuked the winds and sea' before His disciples perished, but the 'Calm' of November 11th, 1918 followed terrible agony and bloodshed. To this the poem pays lip-service as it does, too, to the pity of war:

> *There had been years of Passion—scorching, cold*
> *And much Despair, and Anger heaving high,*
> *Care whitely watching, Sorrows manifold,*
> *Among the young, among the weak and old,*
> *And the pensive Spirit of Pity whispered, 'Why?'*

But the Spirits had similarly whispered in *The Dynasts* (first published 1903–1908), to which 'And there was a Great Calm' is surely a postscript. Hardy did not *need* the First World War to enable him to write such lines; academically, he knew of the futility and horror of war; but the Napoleonic wars of *The Dynasts* were historically distant enough for general, universal anti-war conclusions to be drawn. Hardy was both too near to the First World War to see it for the 'vast international tragedy'[9] that it was, and personally too far from the scene of action to see it in terms of compassion for the individual.

For another older poet, Rudyard Kipling, who was forty-nine years old in 1914, the *idea* of war was poetically familiar; soldiers and battles were the themes of many of his poems; the sentiment of romantic patriotism had been given a new slant in 'The Roman Centurion's Song':

> *Legate, I had the news last night—my cohort ordered home*
> *By ship to Portus Itius and thence by road to Rome.*
> *I've marched the companies aboard, the arms are stowed below:*
> *Now let another take my sword. Command me not to go!*
>
> *I've served in Britain forty years, from Vectis to the Wall*
> *I have none other home than this, nor any life at all.*
> *Last night I did not understand, but, now the hour draws near*
> *That calls me to my native land, I feel that land is here.*
>
>   *   * *   *
>
> *For me this land, that sea, these airs, those folk and fields suffice.*
> *What purple Southern pomp can match our changeful Northern skies,*
> *Black with December snows unshed or pearled with August haze—*
> *The clanging arch of steel-gray March, or June's long-lighted days.*
>
>   *   *   *
>
> *Legate, I come to you in tears—My cohort ordered home!*
> *I've served in Britain forty years. What should I do in Rome?*
> *Here is my heart, my soul, my mind—the only life I know.*
> *I cannot leave it all behind. Command me not to go!*[10]

The love of Britain imposed upon the Roman centurion of 300 A.D. was for Kipling a continuing historical fact through which, in 1914, he saw his vision of war, yet it had become oddly twisted. 'The Roman Centurion's Song' expressed a belief in the sanctity of an individual soul; 'For All We Have and Are', the poem with which Kipling greeted the war in 1914, put forward the idea that the individual soul was subservient to the state:

> *For all we have and are,*
> *For all our children's fate,*
> *Stand up and take the war,*
> *The Hun is at the gate!*

>   *   *   *

> *No easy hope or lies*
> *Shall bring us to our goal,*
> *But iron sacrifice*
> *Of body, will, and soul.*
> *There is but one task for all—*
> *One life for each to give.*
> *What stands if Freedom fall?*
> *Who dies if England live?*[10]

Again, in 1914 the sentiment was not merely acceptable, but was common to many people. However, during the next two years it began to wear thin. In a rather brash article entitled 'My First Week in Flanders', Lieutenant the Hon. W. Watson-Armstrong gave an account of the battle of St. Julien, finishing up by referring to Kipling's poem:

> The other battalions in the brigade all suffered heavily, and our Brigadier himself was killed. On all this, we can only comment that it was the 'fortune of war', and what does it matter who dies, if only England lives?[11]

But to many people it was beginning to matter. His query was answered four months later by E. S. P. Haynes in a memorial article for Alfred and Rupert Brooke and 'Ben' Keeling:

> The sense of loss to England in the death of all these young men must surely obliterate all the old romantic nonsense about war for several decades at least . . . 'Who dies if England lives?' like most rhetorical questions invites no answer. But one may well ask what sort of England would survive if wars on the present scale occurred in each decade.[12]

Yet the attitudes which informed 1914 cannot be judged in the light of understanding which several years of war threw upon events, nor in the perspective of more than sixty years later. The truth for the men of 1914 was that, at the outset, war offered romance and adventure, and the emotions which inspired the men of 1914 are reflected in the romantic poetry of the war:

> *Now, God be thanked Who has matched us with His hour,*
> *And caught our youth, and wakened us from sleeping.*[13]

In what ways did the 'romance of war' manifest itself between 1914 and 1918? First and foremost was the unwonted excitement and exhilaration of living dangerously, of pushing the old life behind and starting afresh; secondly there was an idealistic patriotism which, viewed widely, embraced the whole of England, or viewed more narrowly showed itself in the love of a village or a county, or in the pride of a regiment; thirdly, there was a belief in the glory and honour of acquitting oneself well in battle and this belief culminated in the idea that death in battle was the most fitting and honourable end to life.

The first reaction to war was a sense of release, of excitement and adventure, for during the previous decade there had been no outlet for such feelings. The early years of the century were years in which the prevailing tone was that of security, and with security came lethargy; so much had been achieved in the preceding era that it seemed there was little left to be achieved; the nineteenth century had been one of amazing scientific progress, of tremendous social reforms, of great statesmen and politicians, of powerful writers and thinkers; now the impulse was to rest on these achievements: 'Surely', wrote C. E. Montague,

> there never was any time in the life of the world when it was so good, in the way of obvious material comfort, to be alive and fairly well-to-do as it was before the war.[14]

Yet there was something missing. 'Material comfort' there may have been, but spiritual alertness and stimulus were lacking. To the boys who were growing into manhood during the years before 1914 it seemed that adventure had passed them by. They looked for a challenge and none presented itself. Their spirits seemed to stagnate in the calm of the opening twentieth century. Robert Nichols expressed part of their frustration when he spoke of the security which prevented his contemporaries from being able to 'experience the sensation . . . of carrying [their] soul in [their] teeth'.[15] Those who were unable to live in the imagination were unable to live a life of full awareness, and even the more imaginative looked nostalgically back to their childhood for the life of adventure:

30

Great days we've known, when fancy's barque unfurled
Her faery wings, and bore us through the world
To spy upon the devious ways of men.

*   *   *

For magic ruled the whole earth over then.
Earth was a treasure house of wondrous things.[16]

As men looked at the world around them they could see nothing in the time that appeared to offer an outlet to the spirit, no 'cause on earth for which we might have died' as Newbolt put it in his poem, 'Peace'. Yet the second decade of the century showed how very precarious were the beliefs in peace, safety and security. Certainly 1914 put an end to all such thoughts, and there was an upsurge of excitement which caused the advent of war to be hailed with enthusiasm. Not that people were not anxious during the vital days before the 4th of August to avert war if it were possible. Before the Declaration had been made few people would have chosen war; the daily newspapers expressed the unwillingness of English people to embark upon a European war. On 2/3 August 1914 'Ben' Keeling was writing to his mother-in-law, 'Has ever a nation gone into war more cold-bloodedly and reluctantly than we are going . . . I am amazed at the lack of feeling and interest about the war everywhere—even now'.[17] Yet there was a feeling of inevitability about the whole process. France and Belgium had to fight and if war was coming to such near neighbours, Britain had to fight too, to keep the war away from her own shores. Apart from all matters of policy, the people of France and Belgium were our friends and we could not stand by and see them go under: 'The one topic is—"Are we coming in?" It will be a black shame if we do not stand by our friends,' wrote Douglas Herbert Bell in his Diary for the 3rd of August 1914.

So war came, and the people shouted in the streets and held up the traffic in order to hear the Proclamation of War read. Doubts were dispelled overnight. There was no thought of what war meant, but an overwhelming desire to put the presumptuous German Kaiser in his place, to right the wrongs done to the small countries of Europe, and to show a Britain still victorious and free; and amongst the young men who rushed to enlist there was a feeling inspired by neither patriotism nor duty, but by the knowledge that here at last was a challenge for the dying spirit, here was a cause to fight for, and if necessary to die for. Sir Philip Gibbs, then a young and exceedingly frank and outspoken war-correspondent, understood this attitude and wrote of it in *Now It can Be Told*:

> Some of them offered their bodies because of the promise of a great adventure—and life had been rather dull in office and factory and on the farm. Something stirred in their blood—an old call to youth. Some instinct of a primitive, savage kind, for open air life, fighting, killing, the comradeship of hunters, violent emotions, the chance of death, surged up into the brains of quiet boys, clerks, mechanics, miners, factory hands.[18]

It was true. Boys and young men who had been content to live peaceful and uneventful lives flocked to enlist.

Every daily paper contained letters written by men in the fighting forces rejoicing in their own good fortune and commiserating with their friends and relations who were missing the war. Typical of many letters is this extract from the letter of a serving midshipman to his parents, published in *The Times* for the 11th of November 1914:

> It is awful for Reg being kept at Harrow while this is going on, but I have written to try and cheer him up by saying the war is certain to last two years, by which time he will be able to join in.

Douglas Herbert Bell and his friends in his Territorial Regiment saw the war as 'a bit of a game'[19] and 'Ben' Keeling, in an article published in the *New Statesman* on the 5th of December 1914 wrote,

> I may possibly live to think differently; but at the present moment, assuming this war had to come, I feel nothing but gratitude to the gods for sending it in my time.

Alan Seeger, the American poet, who joined the French Foreign Legion at the outbreak of war, wrote in a letter to his mother on the 17th of October 1914, 'I go into action with the lightest of light hearts ... I am happy and full of excitement over the wonderful days that are ahead'; and again, nearly a week later,

> I am feeling fine, in my element, for I have always thirsted for this kind of thing, to be present always where the pulsations are liveliest. Every minute here is worth weeks of ordinary experience.

About the same time Julian Grenfell wrote to his mother, 'I adore

War. It is like a big picnic without the objectlessness of a picnic. I have never been so well or so happy,'[20] and a week or so later he claimed that 'it is all *the* best fun. I have never felt so well, or so happy, or enjoyed anything so much'.[20] Robert Nichols summed up the attitude to the war of the majority of his contemporaries when he wrote,

> I am surprised looking back, at the lack, as the threat of war intensified, of a feeling of horror—the chief feeling in 1914, you know, was one of extreme and somewhat elevating excitement.[21]

and again,

> In 1914 my generation didn't consider themselves victims—not at all! On the contrary we felt we were in some sort privileged. 'Bliss was it in that dawn to be alive, but to be young was very heaven!'[22]

It was this spirit which inspired the romantic poetry of the early war years. Men who fought in that war and are able to look back to a time before the horrors of attrition set in, seem to be agreed that Rupert Brooke's '1914' sonnets admirably caught the mood of the time and reflected the feelings of most men at the outset of war. Of them Robert Nichols wrote, '. . . they seem to me now, as then, a just, dazzling and perfect expression of what we then felt'.[23] A. J. P. Taylor commented that, 'Rupert Brooke spoke for an entire generation',[24] and Sir Herbert Read, quoting the first of the sonnets in 'Extracts from a War Diary' for the 12th of April 1917, stated,

> But England of these last few years has been rather cold and weary, and one finds little left standing amid the wreckage of one's hopes. So one is glad to leap into the clean sea of danger and self-sacrifice . . . If I do die, it's for the salvation of my own soul; cleansing it of all its little egotisms by one last supreme egotistic act.[25]

This comment so late in the war is surprising, for although the romantic attitude persisted among those who did not go to war until its later stages, Read joined up early in 1915 and went to France later the same year.

From the point of view of his contemporaries, then, Brooke was the voice of their own feelings. What he was expressing was a truth, albeit a transient truth. He was not alone. In a poem which is by no means blind to more permanent truths, Charles Sorley, nevertheless tried to catch some of the inconsequential gaiety and excitement of the marching troops:

> All the hills and vales along
> Earth is bursting into song
> And the singers are the chaps
> Who are going to die perhaps.
>
> *   *   *
>
> From the hills and valleys earth
> Shouts back the sound of mirth,
> Tramp of feet and lilt of song
> Ringing all the road along.
> All the music of their going,
> Ringing swinging glad song-throwing.[26]

Julian Grenfell developed this theme in his poem 'Into Battle', a great paean of rejoicing at the challenge of war:

> The naked earth is warm with Spring,
>   And with green grass and bursting trees
> Leans to the sun's gaze glorying,
>   And quivers in the sunny breeze;
>
> And life is colour and warmth and light,
>   And a striving evermore for these;
> And he is dead who will not fight;
>   And who dies fighting has increase.
>
> *   *   *
>
> And when the burning moment breaks,
> '   And all things else are out of mind,
> And only joy of battle takes
>   Him by the throat, and makes him blind,
>
> Through joy and blindness he shall know,
>   Not caring much to know, that still
> Nor lead nor steel shall reach him, so
>   That it be not the Destined Will.[27]

This was written in Flanders in April 1915. A month later Grenfell was dead. His death, no doubt, added a certain amount of spurious fame to the poem, but any sentimentalizing of his words was unnecessary; it is a good, perhaps a great poem. The enlargement of the spirit which it suggests is reinforced by the life-giving images—Spring, bursting into joyous rebirth, overcomes death, and the excitement of life lived to the full makes fear unnecessary. It is a sentiment with universal application, easy for us to sympathize with in our more reckless moods.

It is indeed incontrovertible that during the first two years of war, up to the beginning of the Battle of the Somme, men's attitudes were ambivalent. While the horror of battle was in no way diminished, many men found the actual experience exhilarating:

> Psychology on the Somme was not simple and straightforward. Men were afraid, but fear was not their dominating emotion, except in the worst hours. Men hated this fighting, but found excitement in it, often exaltation, sometimes an intense stimulus of all their senses and passions before reaction and exhaustion.[28]

This fact has often failed to be recognized and the result has frequently been a condemnation of the romantic poetry of 1914 to 1916. Yet such poetry was reflecting what men were thinking and saying in those early war years, and had the war ended in 1916 Sassoon's savage satire and Owen's suffering realism would have been unknown. By mid-1916 most of the writers quoted above were dead, the years of disillusion and moral bewilderment unknown to them. The ones who remained were writing very differently before the war ended.

The second theme of the romanticists was patriotism. Again, the existence of such a sentiment has been denied. There is a world of difference, however, between Isaac Rosenberg's personal denial in a letter to Edward Marsh, 'I never joined the army from patriotic reasons'[29] and Robert Graves's categorical rejection of the theme: 'Patriotism. There was no patriotism in the trenches. It was too remote a sentiment, and rejected as fit only for civilians.'[30] Graves was wrong. For many men patriotism was an important contributory factor in their attitude to war and this is apparent in many letters home; 'I always feel that I am fighting for England, English fields, lanes, trees, English atmospheres, and good days in England' wrote Lieutenant C. C. Carver in a letter to his brother as late as the 27th of February 1917[31], and Captain J. L. T. Jones wrote to his family of 'fighting for the country which has sheltered and nurtured one all through life'[32].

As an abstract ideal patriotism was comparatively unimportant and as such it was certainly discredited later in the war, but the love of England was frequently put forward as a personal justification for taking part in the war. One cannot fight long for an abstraction, but the idea of defending home and friends, the English 'way of life' was strong and was very frequently interpreted in terms of death; in other words, men were moved and inspired by the thought of dying for their country. So Francis Grenfell writing of his twin brother Riversdale's death commented, 'Rivy died for old England, and no Englishman could do more'[33]. Directly akin to this comment are the final lines of W. N. Hodgson's poem, 'Reverie', in which he described the dead who,

> loving as none other
> The land that is their mother,
> Unfaltering renounced her
> Because they loved her so.

Yet, whilst Francis Grenfell could perhaps justifiably write with assurance of his twin brother's feelings, Hodgson's poem falls into the category of 'sentimental': the cloying 'loving . . . mother . . . loved her so' attempts to evoke a false patriotism by its comparison with a son's love for his mother; as a general statement, even at the outset of war, it is unacceptable. On the other hand, Brooke's best-known sonnet, 'The Soldier', is a more personal, though perhaps a more conceited view of the same sentiment. The death that he romanticizes about is his own and, caught up in the excitement of 1914, he feels himself ready to die for England.

At this time there was no view to take other than the romantic one. Even Edmund Blunden, who is not associated with the romantic attitude, asserts that at the time Brooke was writing 'the romantic note was justified'; he enlarges thus:

At first, speaking broadly, the poetry thus called into existence was concerned with the beauty of English life, made distinct by the act of separation, renunciation. The fact of war was still strange and enigmatic. . . . Hardly anyone could be genuinely, at that early stage, in two minds about it. The appalling destruction which it would ultimately mean, direct and indirect, was not seen. . . . So, the early war poetry is mainly insistent on chivalrous obligation, and home pictures of the life that the soldier leaves behind him.[34]

It was in this spirit that Geoffrey Howard looked back towards England, seeing her as

> very small and very green
> And full of little lanes all dense with flowers
> That wind along and lose themselves between
> Mossed farms, and parks, and fields of quiet sheep.[35]

The theme was popular among minor poets. It reflected the thoughts of most combatants. What they held on to was an anguished love for the things of home, the peace, the quiet, the happiness that life in England represented, as opposed to the disorder, noise and misery of life in war-time France.

The final and most persistent theme of romantic war poetry was that of the glory and honour accruing to those who die in battle. It is a time-honoured theme in English poetry, but also one which appears to have had substance in the minds of the soldiers fighting during the war. Death and the idea of death was in most soldiers' minds, though in the early war years few of them had fully faced up to its reality. Siegfried Sassoon, recalling his thoughts on receiving a letter offering him a commission, wrote,

> As I sat on the ground with my half-cleaned saddle and the War Office letter, I felt very much a man dedicated to death. And to one who had never heard the hiss of machine-gun bullets there was nothing imaginatively abhorrent in the notion.[36]

Neither was it an isolated thought, for a little later he returned to the same theme with, 'In an emotional mood I could glory in the idea of the supreme sacrifice'.[37] To begin with, death was an accepted possibility and was rarely repulsive. Diaries, journals and letters refer to the writer's death without qualms, without sentimentality and almost objectively as though death is simply another milestone in his life: 'Of course in a war of this magnitude and difficulty' wrote Donald Hankey to his sister on the 25th of April 1915 'the chances of coming back are not very great'. Viewed in this abstract way death was not something to be feared, but rather, perhaps, to be gloried in. On the 3rd of July 1915 Alan Seeger, whose attitude to the war continued to be ultra-romantic, wrote to his mother that

> The fears for those who take part in [the war] and who do not return should be sweetened by the sense that their death was the death which

beyond all others they would have chosen for themselves, that they went to it smiling and without regret, feeling that whatever value their continued presence in the world might be to humanity, it could not be greater than the example and inspiration they were to it in so departing.

It was a plea that she should not mourn for him, for death appeared to him in no way abhorrent. Similarly, but much later in the war, 2nd Lt. G. R. Morgan wrote to his father,

> I do not fear Death itself; the Beyond has no terrors for me. I am quite content to die for the cause for which I have given up nearly three years of my life.[38]

This was the romantic view of death current among those 'who had never heard the hiss of machine-gun bullets'. It was faithfully reflected in the romantic poems of the period. Brooke's famous sonnet, 'The Soldier', gained instant popularity because of the large and magnificent acceptance of death which it portrayed. Robert Nichols looked theatrically upon himself going to war and embodied his thoughts in a somewhat over-sentimental poem saying goodbye to his old home and to life:

> *For the last time, maybe, upon the knoll*
> *I stand. The eve is golden, languid, sad . . .*
> *Day like a tragic actor plays his rôle*
> *To the last whispered word, and falls gold-clad.*
> *I, too, take leave of all I ever had.*[39]

Nichols clearly over-reacted to the situation. He was still far from battle and death and the histrionic quality of his words is paralleled in the poem by the rôle he assigns to sunset. Close to the conflict and with knowledge of battle in his heart, W. N. Hodgson began his poem, 'Before Action' with the same image of sunset, but for him it was not play-acting: death appeared imminent and the carelessness with which sunsets had 'spilled' red over the sky reminded him of the random way in which battle 'spilled' blood—soon, he believed, his own:

> *I that on my familiar hill*
> *   Saw with uncomprehending eyes*
> *A hundred of thy sunsets spill*
> *   Their fresh and sanguine sacrifice,*

> *Ere the sun swings his noonday sword*
> *Must say goodbye to all of this;—*
> *By all delights that I shall miss,*
> *Help me to die, O Lord.*

Alan Seeger lacked the certainty of death which appears to have inspired Hodgson, but he nevertheless embraced its possibility in his poetry, just as he had in his letters home:

> *I have a rendezvous with Death*
> *At some disputed barricade.*
>
> *   *   *
>
> *It may be he shall take my hand*
> *And lead me into his dark land*
> *And close my eyes and quench my breath—*
> *It may be I shall pass him still.*[40]

Most poems of this personal kind were written before their writers had seen action, as were most of the letters, diaries and other reminiscences which contain similar remarks. (To this generalization Hodgson's poem is an exception.) Such a condition did not, however, apply to poems written about the death of others. This was, indeed, the last illusion—that one's friends and comrades died gloriously; that, for them, death in battle was heroic and honourable. It perhaps seemed that to shatter this illusion was to dishonour the dead and that it was ignoble to fail to glorify the death in battle of one's friends —as though one thus failed in one's duty towards the dead. Revulsion came later.

W. N. Hodgson described the death of his friend soon after the outbreak of war as being, 'Perfect in one great act of sacrifice'.[41] Almost a year later, Charles Sorley, who was certainly far from being a romantic, wrote in his epitaph to 'S.C.W.' that there could be 'no fitter end' than death in battle and claimed for his dead friend, 'A glory that can never die'. Even in the months after the Somme the lingering illusion remained. Robert Nichols, invalided out of the army, his nerves shattered, ended one of his memorial poems to H. S. Gough, 'Boy', with the lines,

> *What need of comfort has the heroic soul?*
> *What soldier finds a soldier's grave is chill?*[42]

In 1917 Richard Aldington, who viewed with anguish and bitterness

the slaughter of the war, romanticized and idealized the death of one
of his officers in 'Epitaph. 1. H.S.R. Killed April 1917';

> *You are dead—*
> *You, the kindly, courteous,*
> *You whom we loved,*
> *You who harmed no man*
> *Yet were brave to death*
> *And died that other men might live.*[43]

The belief that some soldiers died in order that 'other men might
live' contained its own truth. *How* they died was another story and
was told later in the war.

It is clear then that romantic poetry was a true reflection of what
men were saying, thinking and writing in the early days of the war;
that it represented a phase, but a genuine phase, through which
the majority of men engaged in the war went; that it mirrored the
times, if only briefly, and that it must thus be allowed to take its
place in the course of English poetry, however reluctant we may
be to place it as war poetry beside that of Sassoon and Owen. War
is not, of course, something to be romantic about. This is obvious
to us in the 1970's; it was not so obvious to the men of 1914. To them
what was here and now was truth and in August 1914 the here and
now of war was excitement and exhilaration. It was not until 1917
that Owen demonstrated the need for poetic truth to be absolute
and three years of bitter agony and bloodshed separated 1914 from
the understanding vouchsafed to Owen and his peers.

·CHAPTER·TWO·

❧⟐❧⟐❧⟐❧

The mind is its own place, and in itself
Can make a Heaven of Hell, a Hell of Heaven.

A GREAT DEAL of poetry was written during the war which appeared to have little direct relation to war itself. Most of this was written by non-combatant poets who isolated themselves from the conflict both physically and mentally, and often morally as well. What they wrote has no more connection with the First World War than the mere accident of having been written during the years 1914–1918. It is, however, of some interest to consider why two of the greatest poets of the early twentieth century were silent about the war, for both W. B. Yeats and T. S. Eliot were writing poetry during the war years.

For Yeats, not to write war poetry was a deliberate choice. Born in 1865, he was the same age as Kipling, but his poetry and personal interests had followed very different lines. By 1914 he had published six volumes of poems. His themes were mainly romantic—love, beauty, sorrow, time and the changes brought about by time, Irish mythology, and in his last two volumes, *The Green Helmet and Other Poems* (1910) and *Responsibilities* (1914) there was a growing awareness of contemporary problems in art, literature, the theatre and in Irish affairs. It might perhaps have been expected that this growing awareness would be developed in poems concerned with the European war. However, Yeats, both as an Irishman and as a man too old to be personally involved in the war, judged himself unfit to comment upon the conflict, as he explained in his 'On Being Asked for a War Poem':

> *I think it better that in times like these*
> *A poet's mouth be silent, for in truth*
> *We have no gift to set a statesman right;*
> *He has had enough of meddling who can please*
> *A young girl in the indolence of her youth*
> *Or an old man upon a winter's night.*[1]

At this time Yeats was absorbedly interested in his own art and it is clear that he could not write of the war out of his own experiences or emotions. Had he written war poetry it would have been for some purpose outside himself. Life for Yeats was never straightforward, but was made up of a series of choices in which man and artist often found themselves at variance. Yet his artistic integrity compelled him towards the choices in which he fulfilled himself as a poet. Thus, the total rejection of 'meddling' in politics by writing war poetry was his own choice. Most of the poems in *The Wild Swans at Coole* (1919) and a number of those in *Michael Robartes and the Dancer* (1921) were written during the war, but they can hardly be said to reflect any 'attitude' to the war on Yeats's part. 'Sixteen Dead Men' makes a bare mention of the war; 'In memory of Major Robert Gregory', although an elegy for a friend killed in the war, approaches war only through the indirect and romantic description of

> *my dear friend's dear son,*
> *Our Sidney and our perfect man.*

In fact, the only 'war' poem published in the *Collected Poems*, 'An Irish Airman Foresees His Death', is interesting in that, whilst it is ostensibly connected with the war, its approach is purely an emotional one which directly rejects political or patriotic motivation. This poem also was written for Robert Gregory and admirably captures the spirit of knight-errantry with which he chose to sacrifice his life. It can be considered as an 'escapist' poem in the true sense, for it depicts Gregory in what is essentially a war situation, yet with his mind so absorbed by a new sensation of delight that he can dwell only on the emotional experience:

> *I know that I shall meet my fate*
> *Somewhere among the clouds above;*
> *Those that I fight I do not hate,*
> *Those that I guard I do not love;*
> *My country is Kiltartan Cross,*

> *My countrymen Kiltartan's poor,*
> *No likely end could bring them loss*
> *Or leave them happier than before.*
> *Nor law, nor duty bade me fight,*
> *Nor public man, nor cheering crowds,*
> *A lonely impulse of delight*
> *Drove to this tumult in the clouds;*
> *I balanced all, brought all to mind,*
> *The years to come seemed waste of breath,*
> *A waste of breath the years behind*
> *In balance with this life, this death.*

The Variorum Edition of Yeats's poems contains another poem
not published in his lifetime, which appears to be an answer, or
second thoughts, on the theme of the Irish airman. In this poem the
airman, like Yeats's friend Robert Gregory, is dead after having
brought down 'Some nineteen German planes'; yet at Kiltartan Cross
'Half-drunk or whole-mad soldiery' are running amok in the struggle
between his own people and the nation for which he chose to fight.
Yeats's concern is for Ireland, not for Europe, and his bitter last
words to the airman urge him to

> *close your ears with dust and lie*
> *Among the other cheated dead.*

It is hardly a war poem, yet, such as it is, it is not surprising that Yeats
himself did not publish it for he maintained his objection to war as a
subject for poetry for the rest of his life; when he edited *The Oxford
Book of Modern Verse* in 1935 he almost entirely omitted the war
poets, including only four poems about the war: W. W. Gibson's
'Breakfast', Julian Grenfell's 'Into Battle', Herbert Read's 'The End
of a War' and Siegfried Sassoon's 'On Passing the New Menin Gate'.
In the Introduction he claimed that

> passive suffering is not a theme for poetry....
>
> If war is necessary, or necessary in our time and place, it is best to
> forget its suffering as we do the discomfort of fever, remembering our
> comfort at midnight when our temperature fell.

It seems an extraordinary and scarcely excusable attitude on the part
of a man who lived unscathed through the years of war.

For Eliot the decision not to write war poetry appears to have been
absolute, though less deliberate than Yeats's choice. Born in 1888

he was roughly contemporary with many of the men who were fighting and dying on the various war fronts. He was, of course, an American citizen, and America did not enter the war until 1917. Nevertheless, throughout the whole of the war period Eliot was resident in England, and though it was not until 1927 that he became a British subject, the heritage of English literature already made him look on Britain as his own land. Yet *Prufrock and Other Observations* published in 1917 shows no overt preoccupation with war or war-time conditions. This is, in fact, not surprising, since it is now clear that the more important poems which appeared in the Prufrock volume, including 'The Love Song' itself, date from the period 1910–12. Yet who, reading 'The Waste Land', published in 1922 can doubt that in some profound way the war bit deep into Eliot's consciousness? If he rejected the direct poetic enactment of it he was deeply impressed by the spiritual stagnation and sterility which accompanied four years of massive destruction of human values:

> *Shall I at least set my lands in order?*
> *London Bridge is falling down falling down falling down.*[2]

*　　　　*　　　　*

There are few poems written by those involved in the struggle which show a complete dissociation from it, for it was impossible for most men to divorce their minds from the deeper spiritual involvement: 'Wrote a poem on the Colliery Disaster: but I get mixed up with the war at the end,' remarked Wilfred Owen in a letter to his mother.[3] Though his subject was ostensibly not war, his poem became, nevertheless, a war poem.

The attempt to look outwards, away from the war, is often described as 'escapism', yet it was rarely a genuine escape, but rather, a partial repression. It had to be learned in some measure if sanity was to be retained, but behind it was a lurking awareness of reality. 'We are learning to be soldiers slowly', wrote Charles Sorley a year after the outbreak of war,—'that is to say, adopting the soldierly attitude of complete disconnection with our job during odd hours. No shop'.[4]

Despite the apparent 'soldierliness' of this attitude it was inspired less often by the desire to be unquestioning and loyal soldiers than by the great overwhelming need for the mind to escape from a situation which was well nigh intolerable to men with imagination and sensitivity. The ravages of war had torn to pieces the natural landscape,

44

had disrupted normal human relationships and had demanded from civilized men behaviour which only differed from that of brute beasts in that it excelled theirs in cunning, in cruelty and in compass. To escape from such thoughts men turned to things which could distract them—often momentarily, to sexual satisfaction in the sordid brothels which sprang up in every village or town in Belgium and northern France where soldiers were billeted, and which are alluded to so often in writings of the time; more lastingly, to eternal nature, to distant unchanged homes, to love and friendship. Of these distractions the first has no genuine place in literature; it was without emotion and without passion, a bestial excrescence of the times, a kind of revenge upon Fate who, nevertheless all too often, even in this, had the last laugh: '. . . venereal hospitals at the base were always crowded', wrote Robert Graves.[5]

The second form of distraction was of the mind and of the spirit and its clearest expression is to be found in the poetry written in the war and at war, yet attempting to look outward from the conflict to peace, happiness and security. Yet such an escape was only partial; and it was not confined to poets or poetry, for they were merely giving more intensity to an attitude that was part of the life of many, indeed of most men in the trenches. While beauty and freedom were being destroyed men turned to the natural beauty and freedom of nature as something stable and lasting in the midst of insecurity, for the things of nature defied war: flowers sprang up where towns had been ruined; birds sang while guns roared; the same stars twinkled above friend and enemy alike, over the terrible battlefields of Belgium and France, over England, over Germany. As D. H. Bell noted in his diary for the 8th of February 1915, 'The stars are your only companions on sentry duty in the trenches; and they seem filled with majesty and peace, as does the sunrise too'. Yet, while escaping from the scene around him, some part of his thoughts is still dominated by war: the distant, inaccessible stars are filled with 'peace' which compels the realization that there is no peace on earth.

The references to birds and flowers in every form of writing which came out of the trenches are innumerable. A month after he had written the words quoted above D. H. Bell wrote that it was

a beautiful warm spring afternoon, though misty; and the robins, thrushes, and tits are nesting, and singing as if they were English. Only there are no primroses to 'take the winds of March with beauty' nor any sign of bluebells.[6]

In this context 'as if they were English' detracts from the lyric quality of the scene. Negatively it throws us back to the fact that they are not English; that the scene itself is not in England, but in war-ravaged France; that it is remarkable because it contrasts with what the soldier daily experiences. Edmund Blunden

> heard an evening robin in a hawthorn, and in trampled gardens among the refuse of war there was the fairy, affectionate immortality of the yellow rose and blue-grey crocus.[7]

Again the escape is incomplete: not only are the gardens trampled, and the 'refuse of war' lying around, but the 'immortality' of the flowers serves to remind of the only too certain mortality of soldiers, contrasted in their khaki and field-grey with the yellow and blue-grey of the rose and the crocus.

It was impossible for the mind to escape for long or with any depth of concentration from the war, yet most soldiers encouraged their thoughts to range freely over anything that could pleasantly distract them, so that 'writing in a trench not very far from the Germans' Theodore Wilson described how he could see

> a great blazing belt of yellow flowers . . . smelling to heaven like incense, in the sun—and above it all are more larks. Then a bare field strewn with barbed wire—rusted to a sort of Titian red—out of which a hare came just now, and sat up with fear in his eyes and the sun shining red through his ears. Then the trench.[8]

'Complete disconnection', in Sorley's words, appears to have been rare, but occasional or partial disconnection was common. Images of war were curiously entwined with dissociated thoughts either subconsciously, or, as in the letter above, more deliberately. In this letter a change of focus from the flowers, the sun and the larks brings the field of war into vision, bare of flowers, littered with barbed wire and the wire itself rusted red; then the two scenes coalesce: an image from nature is superimposed upon the war-field, a hare, symbolic of hunted frightened creatures appears; like the soldiers he has 'fear in his eyes', and the sun illuminates his ears to the colour of blood.

Herbert Read saw nature round him as firmly presaging the ills of war:

> Spring we do have here, but in an abortive sort of way. The felled trees bloom, but for the last time, and forget-me-nots spring up among the

ruins. But everything is sad, and our few flowers are like wreaths among so much desolation.[9]

The passage is heavy with doom. Even the first clause of the first sentence has to be assertive, as though the possibility of spring coming is in doubt. The melancholy pattern of 'denial-words' running through the passage: 'abortive . . . felled trees . . . the last time . . . the ruins . . . everything is sad' culminates in the vision of the spring flowers as wreaths, a reminder that the writer is indeed describing a land of death.

Once in France partial disengagement of his mind was probably the most a soldier could hope for. Certainly there are few genuine poems which achieve more than partial disengagement. There are many, however, which gather up the small delights which even trench-warfare was unable to destroy completely. Edward Tennant discovered a garden which had survived the bombardment of Laventie:

> Green gardens in Laventie!
>   Soldiers only know the street
> Where the mud is churned and splashed about
>   By battle-wending feet;
> And yet beside one stricken house there is a glimpse of grass,
>   Look for it when you pass.
>
> Beyond the Church whose pitted spire
>   Seems balanced on a strand
> Of swaying stone and tottering brick
>   Two roofless ruins stand,
> And here behind the wreckage where the back wall should have been
>   We found a garden green.[10]

He saw the gardens and the mud, the shelled house and the grass, in close juxtaposition, and the survival of nature seemed to him a sign of hope, something to be searched out and cherished in the midst of destruction and ruin. The poem is an 'anthology' piece of patchy merit, but it recaptures a fleeting moment, and the disturbed haste of the rhythm of the fifth lines in each stanza is harmonized in the sixth lines, just as the soldiers' disturbed thoughts are harmonized by the peace of the garden.

In a similar fashion, Isaac Rosenberg, returning to his dug-out after an attack, despairing that, though his life was safe, the future held nothing but threat, heard a lark:

> But hark! Joy—joy—strange joy.
> Lo! heights of night ringing with unseen larks.
> Music showering on our upturned listening faces.
>
> Death could drop from the dark
> As easily as song—
> But song only dropped—[11]

Suddenly the future holds hope again, albeit hope precariously balanced 'Like a blind man's dreams on the sand'. The symbolic song keeps thoughts of war at bay and suggests that despite destruction life and joy will endure.

The lark, in fact, recurs frequently in all the literature of the period and together with the poppy it has come to symbolize the hopes and eternal values that sprang from the Flanders mud. The two are associated again in the well-known poem by John McCrae:

> In Flanders fields the poppies blow
> Between the crosses, row on row,
>   That mark our place; and in the sky
>   The larks, still bravely singing, fly
> Scarce heard amid the guns below.[12]

The red of the poppies is all that is left to represent the red blood of those who died, yet, rising triumphantly over the battlefield and singing despite the thunder of the guns, the larks help to serve as a reminder that the cross is a symbol not merely of mortality but of redemption and of rising again.

The crescendo of the lark's song is well portrayed in the first four lines of a sonnet by J. W. Streets (not a great poet, but one who occasionally produced powerfully evocative lines):

> Hushed is the shriek of hurtling shells: and hark!
> Somewhere within that bit of deep blue sky,
> Grand in his loneliness, his ecstasy,
> His lyric wild and free, carols a lark.[13]

In a moment of silence between the shell-blasts the lark aspires to all that the soldier longs for, culminating in freedom and song.

These poems are not 'escapist' poetry, for the poet is rarely trying to escape from the war; they rather belong to a poetry of 'awareness' in which all the poet's faculties are concentrated on extracting from a life in which spiritual values are degraded, any sign of hope or integrity which can add to human dignity and self-respect. Pervasive thoughts of war are always present, but the poet attempts to look outward and to embrace anything that can remind him of a life cleaner and purer than his life in the trenches. So, for W. N. Hodgson, going back 'to rest' after the Battle of Loos, the things of nature stood out clear and beautiful:

> A leaping wind from England,
>   The skies without a stain,
> Clean cut against the morning
>   Slim poplars after rain,
> The foolish noise of sparrows
>   And starlings in a wood—
> After the grime of battle
>   We know that these are good.[14]

Ford Madox Ford saw war and peace inextricably bound together in the scene around him, but it was the song of the lark that allowed him to escape in daydreams to the happiness of country life in England:

> The French guns roll continuously
> And our guns, heavy, slow;
> Along the Ancre, sinuously,
> The transport wagons go,
> And the dust is on the thistles
> And the larks sing up on high . . .
> But I see the Golden Valley
> Down by Tintern on the Wye.[15]

The insistence on the continuance of life distinct from the war was one way in which men were able to disengage their minds from over-oppressive thoughts of war. A kind of reversal of this process, which at first sight appears to be complete escapism or dissociation can also be seen in some of the poetry. The conscious mind escapes and roves over some other scene apparently distant and separate from war, but reality is all-invasive and the poem presents itself on several levels at once. The supreme example of this is Robert Graves's 'A Boy in Church':

> 'Gabble-gabble . . . brethren . . . gabble-gabble!'
>   My window frames forest and heather.
> I hardly hear the tuneful babble,
>   Not knowing nor much caring whether

The text is praise or exhortation,
Prayer or thanksgiving, or damnation.

Outside it blows wetter and wetter,
    The tossing trees never stay still.
I shift my elbows to catch better
    The full round sweep of heathered hill.
The tortured copse bends to and fro
In silence like a shadow-show.

The parson's voice runs like a river
    Over smooth rocks. I like this church:
The pews are staid, they never shiver,
    They never bend or sway or lurch.
'Prayer,' says the kind voice, 'is a chain
That draws down Grace from Heaven again.'

I add the hymns up, over and over,
    Until there's not the least mistake.
Seven-seventy-one. (Look! there's a plover!
    It's gone!) Who's that Saint by the lake?
The red light from his mantle passes
Across the broad memorial brasses.

It's pleasant here for dreams and thinking,
    Lolling and letting reason nod,
With ugly serious people linking
    Sad prayers to a forgiving God. . . .
But a dumb blast sets the trees swaying
With furious zeal like madmen praying.[16]

The poem contrasts the peaceful security within the church with the wildness of the storm outside, but through his description of the natural storm the poet is analogizing the storms of war. It is only through the discernment of this analogy that the full force of the troubled and violent vocabulary can be felt: the wet and the turbulence of the second stanza lead toward the vision of the 'tortured copse' which is, through sound association, a *tortured corpse* of war from the real (i.e. not the 'shadow-') show. Unlike the dug-outs and the trenches the church is stable and secure; its staid wooden pews contrast with the tossing trees in the storm. The poem culminates in the terrifying futility of a big battle with its 'dumb blast', 'furious zeal' and its realization of men gone mad.

Siegfried Sassoon attempted something of the same sort in 'Haunted', though the whole of this poem is heavy with threat, and the suppression of war thoughts has only succeeded in producing a nightmare theme—a man alone, in a wood, terrified, unable to escape, pursued by some inhuman creature, threatened by louring storm and thunder; but at the same time we know that the man is a soldier caught in a gas attack in No Man's Land, struggling to get back to his own lines and the 'voices of tired men'; sunset has 'Died in a smear of red'; he stumbles through the barbed wire barricades ('Barbed brambles gripped and clawed him round his legs') but is overcome by the gas and falls dying at the end of the poem:

> Then the slow fingers groping on his neck,
> And at his heart the strangling clasp of death.[17]

The two poems quoted above were deliberate attempts on the part of Graves and Sassoon to show how intrusive thoughts of war had become to those involved in it. There seem to be few poems worth preserving which were written by soldiers on active service and which show a complete dissociation from the war. In Books II and III of *Ardours and Endurances*, Robert Nichols published a number of poems which had no relation to his war experiences, but some of them were written before the war and none of them is memorable. His active service was, in fact, of short duration; he was sent home from France in 1916 suffering from shell-shock. A poem such as 'Last Words', though written in April 1916, was written at home. Its sentimentality has lost the poignancy of the earlier poem 'Farewell to Place Of Comfort'; at Lawford in April 1916 it seemed unlikely that a twenty-three year old soldier, home from the front physically unharmed, was soon to die. The Keatsian overtones are too lush:

> O let it be
> Just such an eve as this when I must die!
> To see the green bough soaking, still against a sky
> Washed clean after the rain.
> To watch the rapturous rainbow flame and fly
> Into the gloom where drops fall goldenly,
> And in my heart to feel the end of pain.

Yet in the previous poem he had been close enough to the reality of death and it is strange to find him playing so fancifully with a theme that must surely have reminded him of his comrades left behind in France.

Sassoon too, published in *The Old Huntsman* a number of his early poems; it is difficult to date them precisely, but the style and the choice of subject suggest that the non-war poems pre-date Sassoon's period of active service and again, few of them (with the exception of 'The Old Huntsman') are worth preserving except as they throw light upon Sassoon's poetic progress.

Francis Ledwidge, in two wartime volumes[18] wrote mainly 'escapist' poetry, choosing as his subjects fairies, the Irish countryside, the gentler aspects of nature and sentimental love. His service during the first two years of the war was at home and then in Serbia, Greece and Egypt. Nothing in *Songs of Peace* published in 1917 suggests that his heart was moved by the realities of war. In Serbia he wrote of the night beetles, the moon, autumn, roses, subjects which in 1915 were ultra-romantic. How much the tone of his poems was at variance with the mood of the times can be judged from the final two lines of his last Serbian poem, 'Spring and Autumn':

> *I with desire am growing old*
> *And full of winter pain.*

But 'growing old' was not within the conceptual grasp of most of his fellow-soldiers. More akin to their comprehension and experience were the words of Binyon, asserting

> *They shall grow not old, as we that are left grow old:*
> *Age shall not weary them, nor the years condemn.*[19]

It is, I think, more surprising to find that in 1916 and early 1917 Ledwidge was able to maintain his attitude of complete dissociation, even on the Western Front. But his air of conscious 'separateness' makes his verse seem empty and lacking in vitality:

> *Once more the lark with song and speed*
> *Cleaves through the dawn, his hurried bars*
> *Fall, like the flute of Ganymede*
> *Twirling and whistling from the stars.*
>
> *The primrose and the daffodil*
> *Surprise the valleys, and wild thyme*
> *Is sweet, on every little hill,*
> *When lambs come down at folding time. . . .*

> *And when the blue and gray entwine*
> *The daisy shuts her golden eye,*
> *And peace wraps all those hills of mine*
> *Safe in my dearest memory.*[20]

The concepts of 'peace' and 'safety' were indeed so distant that reference to them exacerbates the triteness of the poem. The lark no longer, as in Rosenberg's poem quoted above, symbolizes the hopeful aspirations of those trapped in the war, but is dealt with as in a literary exercise; truth has been sacrificed to expression: 'song and speed' alliterate, it is true, but is 'speed' an apt or accurate description of the lark's rise skyward? And can the song of the lark be divided into 'bars', or is the word merely used to rhyme with 'stars'?

It is Edward Thomas who at first appears as the 'escapist' poet *par excellence*. His poetry, none of which was written until after his meeting with Robert Frost in October 1913, expresses with great control and economy the serenity and beauty he found in natural things. At the same time there is an unquestionable awareness of the war, occasionally in his choice of subject but more frequently in his choice of vocabulary:

> *The blackthorns down along the brook*
> *With wounds yellow as crocuses . . .* (p. 100)[21]
>
> *a sentry of dark betonies* (p. 75)
>
> *Tall reeds*
> *Like criss-cross bayonets* (p. 59)
>
> *And salted was my food, and my repose,*
> *Salted and sobered, too, by the bird's voice*
> *Speaking for all who lay under the stars,*
> *Soldiers and poor, unable to rejoice.* (p. 26)

Thomas went to France in late January 1917; he was killed in the battle of Arras on the 9th of April 1917. It has been conclusively demonstrated by William Cooke in his critical biography that all Thomas's poetry in fact pre-dates his going to France so that what we see here is the reverse of an escape from the war: the poet is clinging to his own way of life but finding himself increasingly committed to involvement:

> *Now all roads lead to France*
> *And heavy is the tread*
> *Of the living.*

There is no poetry coloured by his trench experiences and it is useless to conjecture what such poetry would have been like.

The one poet who consistently wrote poems which, whilst looking away from the war, nevertheless showed an intense awareness of war-time experience in France was Ivor Gurney. He is a much neglected poet who survived the war a broken man and died in the City of London Mental Hospital on Boxing Day, 1937. He published two war volumes, *Severn and Somme*, 1917 and *War's Embers*, 1919.

A striking feature of many of the poems in these volumes is their similarity to the kind of letters and diary entries quoted above. Even in 'Carol', one of the few non-war poems in *Severn and Somme*, war thoughts are intrusive. Though the poem is to celebrate Christmas, winter is described as having 'Killed with tiny swords' the leaves of the trees; 'All green things . . . have . . . died'; the holly which has withstood winter is 'brave'; along with the shouting, dancing and singing to celebrate Christmas we are called upon to 'Honour courage'.

More commonly, as in 'The Farm' from *War's Embers*, Gurney evokes memories of past scenes and pleasures in order to dispel present fears:

> *A creeper-covered house, an orchard near;*
> *A farmyard with tall ricks upstanding clear*
> *In golden sunlight of a late September.—*
> *How little of a whole world to remember!*
> *How slight a thing to keep a spirit free.*

> *   *   *

> *(When day died out behind the lovely bare*
> *Network of twigs, orchard and elms apart;*
> *When rooks lay still in round dark nests above,*
> *And Peace like cool dew comforted the heart).*[22]

Against a background of a world at war the Harveys' farmhouse was small enough and yet its memory, distinct and separate from war, was able to free the war-bound spirit of the poet; and day could die and darkness come with memories of peace to comfort the heart. For Gurney the evocation of such memories was a conscious effort to escape war fears; the poem 'Contrasts'[23] opens with the following stanza:

> *If I were on the High Road,*
> *That runs to Malvern Town*

> *I should not need to read, to smoke,*
> *My fear of death to drown;*
> *Watching the clouds, skies, shadows dappling*
> *The sweet land up and down.*

and 'De Profundis'[24] has a similar approach:

> *If only this fear would leave me I could dream*
> *of Crickley Hill*
> *And a hundred thousand thoughts of home would*
> *visit my heart in sleep.*

That complete escape was not attainable, is made only too clear by the conditional openings of these two poems, and, in each, thoughts of war swiftly overtake the poet, for both continue with the words 'But here', bursting the dream bubble and presenting the reality: 'But here the shells rush over,/We lie in evil holes,' ('Contrasts') and 'But here the peace is shattered all day by the devil's will' ('De Profundis'). Yet Gurney continued to write poems which, whilst constantly aware of the war, looked outwards to the remembered peace of England and his Gloucestershire home and friends.

Generally, only in so far as judgment is implicit in the contrast between war and peace, did Gurney's poems show any 'anti-war' element. An excellent illustration of this is to be found in 'Trees'.[24] The starting point of this poem is a parenthetical comment in quotation marks:

> ('You cannot think how ghastly these battlefields look under a grey sky. Torn trees are the most terrible thing I have ever seen. Absolute blight and curse is on the face of everything.')

Yet the poet attempts to look outward, away from the scene of war:

> *The dead land oppressed me;*
> *I turned my thoughts away,*
> *And went where hill and meadow*
> *Are shadowless and gay.*
>
> *Where Coopers stands by Cranham,*
> *Where the hill-gashes white*
> *Show golden in the sunshine,*
> *Our sunshine—God's delight.*

> *Beauty my feet stayed at last*
> *Where green was most cool,*
> *Trees worthy of all worship*
> *I worshipped . . . then, O fool,*
>
> *Let my thoughts slide unwitting*
> *To other, dreadful trees, . . .*
> *And found me standing, staring*
> *Sick of heart—at these!*

As usual the escape is all too brief. In a circular movement his mind travels from the battlefield to the hills and meadows of his home; he dwells upon the beauty of sunshine and trees and is unwillingly dragged back again to the battlefield from which he had tried to escape.

Similarly, the 'romance' of war is rarely seen in Gurney's poetry. At times, in fact, he seems at pains to refute it, as in 'De Profundis', the opening lines of which were quoted above:

> *We are stale here, we are covered body and soul and mind*
> *With mire of the trenches, close clinging and foul,*
> *We have left our old inheritance, our Paradise behind,*
> *And clarity is lost to us and cleanness of soul.*
>
> *O blow here, you dusk-airs and breaths of half-light,*
> *And comfort despairs of your darlings that long*
> *Night and day for sound of your bells, or a sight*
> *Of your tree-bordered lanes, land of blossom and song.*

Is it mere coincidence that the vocabulary of this poem bears a resemblance to that used by Brooke in his '1914' sonnets? Or was Gurney in his own way, 'out of the depths', actively denying that experience of war can be romantic? Brooke, in 1914, ended the first of his sonnets with the line, 'And the worst friend and enemy is but Death'. Gurney's answer to Brooke appears to be the line with which he ended 'De Profundis': 'Oh! Death would take so much from us, how should we not fear?'

In *Severn and Somme* there are five sonnets dedicated 'To the Memory of Rupert Brooke'. They are headed simply 'Sonnets 1917' but their writer had lived through three years of war and taken part in the Battle of the Somme since those other five sonnets of 1914 had been written and since Brooke had died. The challenge to Brooke's romanticism is contained in these sonnets written to his memory:

56

> *Though heaven be packed with joy-bewildering*
> *Pleasures of soul and heart and mind, yet who*
> *Would willingly let slip, freely let go*
> *Earth's mortal loveliness . . .?*

That is, the challenge is not one of war realism such as Sassoon and Owen were to make, but one of belief in the survival of the human spirit in conditions which would not lead to the premature destruction of the human body. It is one of the ironies of war that Gurney whose poems repeatedly expressed this belief should become a war casualty not in body, but in mind; that in the midst of death and destruction he could be aware of salvation of the spirit through the contemplation of the enduring beauties of nature, but that when war was over the memory of its horrors had so gripped his mind that he was unable to look outward from his own misery:

> *Horror follows horror within me;*
> *There is a chill fear*
> *Of the storm that does deafen and din me*
> *And rage horribly near.*
>
> *What black things had the human*
> *Race in store, what mind could view—*
> *Good guard the hour that is coming:*
> *Mankind safe, honour bring through.*[25]

or again, 'There are strange Hells within the minds War made'. As far as Ivor Gurney is concerned it is certain that his escape was not merely partial in the usual sense, but was an escape of his conscious mind only.

The attitude to war discussed in this chapter differed from the romantic attitude in that it necessitated the experience of war. Yet it was basically uncritical: if war had to be endured, the spirit could be refreshed by dwelling on things of peace. Death was neither welcome nor glorious, but honour and courage were not devalued.

·CHAPTER·THREE·

Suffering is permanent, obscure and dark,
And shares the nature of infinity.

To UNDERSTAND THE CHANGE of emphasis which took place in the poetry of war during the years 1914–18, it is necessary to understand the changes which influenced men's minds and hearts. For most men who took part in the war and lived through it the pattern of war experience was the same: first, the excitement and enthusiasm of a new adventure; next, the disagreeable surprise when face to face with reality; finally, the terrible cold disillusionment, the full realization of the implications of war and the revulsion from former hopes and beliefs.

When disillusionment came it brought with it no simple way to understanding, no clear-cut path which could be followed by the whole man. Instead it tore men apart, so that they felt they understood nothing. It was this mood of bewilderment and of horror that inspired the 'realist' poetry of the war. This, in its turn, reflected the true thoughts and feelings of men at war, but by now experience had matured and coloured emotion. From trenches and battlefields flowed accounts of what war was and what war meant. Diaries, letters, newspaper reports began to belie the old romantic ideas of war and—more vital, because more permanent—poetry, which had been chief vehicle for romanticism, took on a new hard reality.

The first thing that emerged clearly from all these accounts was the terrible suffering that was to be found everywhere in the war area. Physical distress and misery appeared to be easily communicated for they seemed straightforward and uncomplicated, able to be understood by those who had not seen them. Most writers did not at first realize that their communication was only partial and that the most they could hope for from men and women at home was an academic acceptance of the truth of their words. Robert Nichols put this very clearly and simply in the Introduction to his *Anthology of War Poetry*:

> Were I to say to you 'Fifty pounds of T.N.T. contained in an iron canister will, if detonated in a sufficiently confined space, blow to bits any men present in the space' you would probably only nod. Why? Because 'blown to bits' is a mere phrase; whereas collecting those bits for burial when they have been strewn about a cow-byre is an appalling experience.

Yet accounts of war continued to pour out of France, perhaps because the soldiers hoped that someone would understand them, perhaps because they felt that the truth had to be told whether it was understood or not, perhaps as a form of *catharsis* by which men purged their minds of horrors and helped to keep themselves sane.

The war had hardly begun before reports of cruel physical devastation were being published. For many men in France the romance of war endured for all too brief a time. Already on the 15th of September 1914 a correspondent of *The Times* was writing,

> I have come from Orleans where the hospitals are full of broken men, young men and men in their prime, who have laid youth and strength upon this blood-drenched altar of freedom. I have seen sights too terrible to speak of, sights which I cannot describe—which in the selfishness of his health a man tries to blot from his memory.

These were the words of a non-combatant, but of one writing the truth according to his knowledge, who had seen that the old conventional romantic terms were not sufficient to describe war as it was. He had not completely expunged these terms: he still wrote of youth and strength being 'laid upon the altar of freedom', but it was a blood-drenched altar, suggestive of heathen sacrifice, not the Christian altar, offering renewal of life to those who knelt before it. He was in France, in the war area, and there the war took on the same complexion for all men, experience differing only in the degree of vulnerability of body, mind and spirit.

Writing to his mother a year later a young officer in hospital suffering from shell-shock summed up battle experience as it had seemed to him. He was describing the Battle of Loos; it could have been almost any battle on the western front at any time during the war:

> Nothing could be an exaggeration of the horrors of that battlefield; it was, it is, a veritable shambles, a living death of unspeakable horror even to those who, like myself were, destined to come through it unscathed, bodily at all events. Most of the survivors went through it as through a ghastly nightmare without the relief and joy of awakening.[1]

A year's carnage and the writer's personal involvement in battle have added bitterness to his words. The sacrificial altar has become a slaughter-house, the heroic dream of glory 'a ghastly nightmare'.

There seems little doubt that the words of Robert Nichols quoted above are true in essence. Second-hand experience cannot shatter illusions. Every man had to experience war, real war, for himself, before he could believe that his visions of greatness and glory were false. It is not unusual to be able to trace in diaries and letters the actual process of disillusionment and it was generally physical misery that made the first impact. On the 18th of November 1914 D. H. Bell found himself in support trenches and he and his battalion watched as wounded and broken men returned from the front line, 'incredibly dirty and played out. . . . plastered with mud from head to foot . . . all barely able to drag one foot after another'.[2] Naïvely surprised, the watchers wondered what such ruined shells of men could be and hoped they would never look like that. One senses in Bell's diary entry the lack of understanding and identity with the soldiers who straggled in. Even though he was himself in the trenches he had so far experienced the horrors of war only vicariously. A year later Bell's own personal experiences had made him understand war for what it was. In a diary entry strikingly similar to the one quoted above he reports the relief of his own Brigade from the Front Line:

> It was a shocking sight to see the battalion march into billets when morning came. Pale and weary, plastered from head to foot with white chalk and mud, what was left of them stepped out desperately to the pipers playing. Only two officers who went over the top remain.[3]

This extract gives prominence to one of the miseries of trench warfare which perhaps served more to demoralize most men than fear of physical injury by bullet, grenade or shrapnel: mud and water in the trenches were as sure enemies of the soldiers as the men in the opposing lines and certainly took a heavy toll of life, both directly, by slow drowning and immersion, and indirectly, by preying upon nerves already keyed to breakingpoint. The evidence for the extreme horror with which the soldiers viewed the mud and water in the trenches and in No Man's Land is overwhelming. It was a subject returned to again and again in correspondence throughout the war. 'The trenches here are up to and above our knees in water and sludge', wrote one Territorial officer in a letter later published in *The Times*.[4] Private William Burgon of the 19th Royal Fusiliers in his 1915 Christmas letter to his parents wrote that he and his companions 'were isolated from the other platoons by mud almost impassable and quite uninhabitable'[5]; on the 4th of January 1917, a few days after arriving in France, Wilfred Owen wrote home that he had been 'let down, gently, into the real thing, Mud'. Men confided similar comments to their own private diaries. On the 7th of December 1915 Arthur Graeme West recorded in his diary that the mud and water were 'worse than anything we had ever met'; he added that 'many went in up to their necks, and all of us were soaked up to and over the knees'. Conditions never seemed to improve: in the height of summer, the 29th of June 1917, the Master of Belhaven noted in his Diary, 'I am wet to the waist, and slimy from head to foot—and still the rain comes steadily down'. Other reports tell of men sucked down into the clay and unable to escape from it; 'their fate was not spoken of', commented Edmund Blunden.[6]

The feeling against mud and water appeared to be universal and also dates from most periods of the war except for 1914, but there were many other forms of physical suffering and misery which had to be endured. C. S. Lewis describing his experiences in the trenches during the winter of 1917–18 combined the horror of water with the terrible deprivation of sleep. 'Through the winter, weariness and water were our chief enemies', he commented.[7] Edmund Blunden too, remembered the lack of sleep: 'The great defect of war here as elsewhere was the shortage of sleep',[8] he wrote, and Alexander Caseby noted in his Diary for the 25th of March 1918: 'Men very tired and have poor rations. Want of sleep "tells" on the men.' In *Disenchantment* C. E. Montague enlarged on these statements, asserting that 'most of the privates were tired the whole of the time; sometimes to the point of torment, sometimes much less, but always more or less tired'[9].

To add to the general physical discomfort soldiers and trenches alike were infested by lice, though it appears that many men were more reticent in writing of these in their letters home. Similarly, particularly to the squeamish, the rabbit-sized rats which throve on the unexpected bounty of the war dead were a constant physical terror.

Over and above the conditions of discomfort and misery there were the actual physical results of battle. Shelling and gunfire rarely resulted in the 'nice clean wound' that soldiers prayed for, but rather in horribly wounded and broken men. Those who had seen battle began to confide its horrors to diaries and reports and the terms they used no longer allowed the possibility of 'glory' in war; death was not heroic but ghastly, and was shown as such. For example, on the 25th of April 1915 D. H. Bell wrote in his diary:

> Etched in my brain is the picture of one of our officers lying dead, sprawling on his back, head down, mouth open, eyes staring in the middle of what was once a section of trench, now a jumble of upturned earth and ruptured sandbags.

Three years later Alexander Caseby described in his diary the great retirement from the Somme in Spring 1918:

> This scene was beyond words. Dead, dying and half demented soldiers and civilians lay everywhere, crippled transports and slaughtered animals blocked roads.

In addition to the wounding and death from shell and gunfire there was the even more terrible hazard of gas which left many of those it did not kill maimed and broken. It combined the horrors of physical suffering with those of mental anguish:

> Another officer . . . became delirious and had to be held down. . . . One man underwent the most remarkable muscular contortions, and when he recovered consciousness he was paralysed and was unable to move for some hours. . . . One or two struggled violently, bit the men attending to them and appeared to be temporarily insane.[10]

The 'romance of war' was completely devalued. It had never been more than an idea fostered by history books and literature. The experience of war, certainly war in the trenches on the western front, was frequently too horrible to contemplate; 'God, in Thy mercy, let me never again hear any one speak of the Glory of War!' wrote Ralph Scott in his Diary for the 14th of July 1918.

War had ceased to be a great adventure and it was no longer thought the sportsmanlike thing to conceal its miseries. The accumulation of suffering and horror had to be told, more particularly so because officialdom had realized the necessity of glorifying war if enough men were to be recruited to bring it to a satisfactory political end:

> [The War Office] apprehended that in order to stimulate the recruiting of the New Army now being called to the colours by vulgar appeals to sentiment and passion, it might be well to 'write up' the glorious side of war as it could be seen at the base . . . without, of course, any allusion to dead or dying men, to the ghastly failures of distinguished generals, or to the filth and horror of the battlefields.[11]

A criticism often made of the writings of this period is that the writers lay the horrors on too thick, that they appear to indulge themselves by wallowing in terrifying and brutal description. It is a criticism of hindsight, and perhaps of self-preservation, for such descriptions, read with any understanding or feeling of commitment, must destroy complacency for ever. For the first time in the history of civilization a concerted effort was made by a majority of participants to tell the truth about war and to try to ensure that the truth was remembered. 'The old lie, "Dulce et decorum est pro patria mori"' had re-asserted itself time out of number. The writers of the First World War hoped to suppress it for ever. Professor Bernard Bergonzi suggests in *Heroes' Twilight* in his chapter on Sassoon that exposing 'with sufficient fidelity the nature of death and mutilation in battle' was not a 'sufficient argument against war', but it was nevertheless a powerful argument.

The first task of the realist poet then, was to show what war meant in terms of physical suffering, not to gloss over the agonizing details, and, above all, not to write euphemistically in the old romantic terms which had belied war:

> *Where are the battle-cries,*
> *The flashing eyes,*
> *The flying banners and the spears of Thor?*
> *Here there are only mud, and filth, and flies,*
> *And foul obscenities men's hearts abhor.*[12]

The physical realities of the soldier's life were unlike anything he had ever imagined. In fact, there is little evidence that men when they joined up had given any thought at all to the actual physical conditions of trench warfare. It seems improbable that anyone could have conjured up a vision of the cold, the mud and the lice. The possibility of death occurred to many, if not to most, but death had not meant to them the terrible wounds, the slow choking by gas, the lingering and agonising pain. The letters, diaries and other reports such as those quoted above attempted to state the true facts of war. The poetic presentation of these facts was one of the tasks that poets such as Wilfred Owen and Siegfried Sassoon set themselves. The discomfort of the trenches, deep in mud and water was depicted again and again; Sassoon's graphic description in 'The Redeemer' recaptures the fear and horror of such life:

> Darkness: the rain sluiced down; the mire was deep;
> It was past twelve on a mid-winter night . . .
> We lugged our clay-sucked boots as best we might
> Along the trench; sometimes a bullet sang,
> And droning shells burst with a hollow bang;
> We were soaked, chilled and wretched, every one.

In 'The Sentry' Owen presents us with a similar scene:

> Rain guttering down in waterfalls of slime,
> Kept slush waist-high and rising hour by hour,
> And choked the steps too thick with clay to climb.

Herbert Read, attempted in 'Kneeshaw Goes to War' to focus on the individual human predicament by describing a particularised incident:

> A man who was marching by Kneeshaw's side
> Hesitated in the middle of the mud,
> And slowly sank, weighted down by equipment and arms.
> He cried for help;
> Rifles were stretched to him;
> He clutched and they tugged,
> But slowly he sank.
> His terror grew—
> Grew visibly when the viscous ooze
> Reached his neck.
> And there he seemed to stick,
> Sinking no more.
> They could not dig him out—
> The oozing mud would flow back again.

Mud and slime and water are shown to be not merely the beginnings of discomfort but the cause of inconceivable horrors. Yet all the other physical miseries had to be added to the picture before any true idea of trench conditions could be formed. Sassoon described the return of a Company from the Front Line, emphasizing their utter exhaustion:

> *Up a disconsolate straggling village street*
> *I saw the tired troops trudge: I heard their feet.*
> *The cheery Q.M.S. was there to meet*
> *And guide our Company in . . .*
> > *I watched them stumble*
> *Into some crazy hovel, too beat to grumble.*[13]

Richard Aldington showed the lack of sleep as being an incidental misery, not a part of war itself, but a direct result of war:

> *Four days the earth was rent and torn*
> *By bursting steel,*
> *The houses fell about us;*
> *Three nights we dared not sleep,*
> *Sweating, and listening for the imminent crash*
> *Which meant our death.*
>
> *The fourth night every man,*
> *Nerve-tortured, racked to exhaustion,*
> *Slept, muttering and twitching,*
> *While shells crashed overhead.*[14]

Isaac Rosenberg returned in poetry to his own agonizing burden of horror:

> *I killed them, but they would not die.*
> *Yea! all the day and all the night*
> *For them I could not rest nor sleep,*
> *Nor guard from them nor hide in flight . . .*
>
> *I killed and killed with slaughter mad;*
> *I killed till all my strength was gone.*
> *And still they rose to torture me,*
> *For Devils only die for fun.*
>
> *I used to think the Devil hid*
> *In women's smiles and wine's carouse.*
> *I called him Satan, Balzebub.*
> *But now I call him dirty louse.*[15]

The poets also tried to convey the truth of war by writing of the actual results of battle—terrible wounds, mutilation and physical agony. Herbert Read had become a soldier in a spirit of adventure, but disillusionment soon came to him:

> One week in the trenches was sufficient to strip war of its lingering traces of romance: there was nothing in the Ypres Salient where I first went into the line, but primitive filth, lice, boredom and death.[16]

In his poetry he made it apparent that war was not romantic. The first poem in his war volume, *Naked Warriors*, was 'Kneeshaw Goes to War', an incident from which is quoted above. Like the term 'Naked' in the title of the volume, the name Kneeshaw suggests a vulnerability; it is a half-humorous name, chosen to exclude any possibility of heroic overtones, unromantic and slightly ridiculous. In the poem, Kneeshaw (indeed no hero) ended up 'Minus a leg, on crutches'. Owen's soldier in 'Disabled' has lost both his legs:

> He sat in a wheeled chair, waiting for dark,
> And shivered in his ghastly suit of grey,
> Legless, sewn short at elbow. Through the park
> Voices of boys rang saddening like a hymn,
> Voices of play and pleasure after day,
> Till gathering sleep had mothered them from him.

Though the poem is told in the third person the effect of the last three and a half lines is to place the reader in the position of the disabled soldier and to point the contrast between his expectations and those of the strong and healthy boys in the park. In another of Owen's poems, 'The Chances', a Cockney Tommy lists in a down-to-earth, unsentimental way the results of battle:

> One of us got the knock-out, blown to chops,
> T'other was 'urt, like, losin' both 'is props.
> An' one, to use the word of 'ypocrites,
> 'Ad the misfortoon to be took be Fritz.
> Now me, I wasn't scratched, praise God Amighty
> (Though next time please I'll thank 'im for a blighty).
> But poor young Jim, 'e's livin' an' 'e's not;
> 'E reckoned 'e'd five chances, an' 'e 'ad;
> 'E's wounded, killed, and pris'ner, all the lot,
> The bloody lot all rolled in one. Jim's mad.

Sassoon makes a similar list and also places it in the mouth of a soldier:

> George lost both his legs; and Bill's
> stone blind;
> Poor Jim's shot through the lungs and like
> to die;
> And Bert's gone syphilitic.[17]

It is clear that realism had completely superseded the romantic attitude for those who had had the experience of battle. From this point of view it is interesting here to observe Rudyard Kipling's progress in thought from the trite 'What stands if Freedom fall?/Who dies if England live?' quoted above (p. 29). In 1915 the war touched him personally when his son John was killed in action. His realization of the horror of war was, however, entirely literary:

> The Garden called Gethsemane
> In Picardy it was,
> And there the people came to see
> The English soldiers pass.

> *   *   *

> The Garden called Gethsemane,
> It held a pretty lass,
> But all the time she talked to me
> I prayed my cup might pass.
> The officer sat on the chair
> The men lay on the grass,
> And all the time we halted there
> I prayed my cup might pass.
> It didn't pass—it didn't pass—
> It didn't pass from me.
> I drank it when we met the gas
> Beyond Gethsemane.[18]

The association of Gethsemane with Christ's agony helped Kipling to achieve a reference to the agony of war without being explicit. At the same time, the identification of the suffering soldier with Christ was one which was widely used by the realist poets and which will be discussed later. However, the impact of Kipling's poem is negligible if one compares it with Wilfred Owen's account of a gas attack:

> Gas! Gas! Quick, boys!—An ecstasy of fumbling,
> Fitting the clumsy helmets just in time;
> But someone still was yelling out and stumbling

And flound'ring like a man in fire or lime . . .
Dim, through the misty panes and thick green light,
As under a green sea, I saw him drowning.

In all my dreams before my helpless sight,
He plunges at me, guttering, choking, drowning.

If in some smothering dreams you too could pace
Behind the wagon that we flung him in,
And watch the white eyes writhing in his face,
His hanging face, like a devil's sick of sin;
If you could hear, at every jolt, the blood
Come gargling from the froth-corrupted lungs,
Obscene as cancer, bitter as the cud
Of vile, incurable sores on innocent tongues,—
My friend, you would not tell with such high zest
To children ardent for some desperate glory,
The old Lie: Dulce et decorum est
Pro patria mori.[19]

The realism of this poem is particularly horrible and frightening. It has an immediacy which conveys the panic which occurred when a gas attack began. Nothing in the poem is irrelevant or can allow misinterpretation—no garden, no suggestion of redemption by impli- cation, no possibility of choice. In Kipling's poem, the title itself, 'Gethsemane', and the use of words suggest the possibility of choice at least insofar as Christ had a choice, 'O my Father, if it be possible, let this cup pass from me: nevertheless, not as I will, but as thou wilt'. Even this is denied to Owen's gassed soldiers—the cup is not offered to them to drink; they are unwillingly smothered, immersed, drowned in the poison which Kipling's soldier politely quaffs down to his own destruction. Owen was a combatant re-interpreting war for the non-combatant, determined that lies should be known as lies and that the truth, however horrible, should be told to those who were unaware of it, and that the understanding of truth began with the knowledge of physical suffering on a scale such as had never been known before.

It has already been suggested that the idea to which romantic notions attached themselves most persistently and most perseveringly was that of the glory and honour belonging to death in battle. For the idea to be perpetuated death had to be seen as clean and immediate, not disgusting and lingering, yet the truth of the majority of deaths in war was quite other than the romantic view. Arthur Graeme West's description of a scene in a trench after a German bombardment is sufficient to dispel illusions about what death in battle is really like:

The trench was a mere undulation of newly-turned earth, under it somewhere lay two men or more. You dug furiously. No sign. Perhaps you were standing on a couple of men now, pressing the life out of them, on their faces or chests. A boot, a steel helmet—and you dig and scratch and uncover a grey, dirty face, pitifully drab and ugly, the eyes closed, the whole thing limp and mean-looking: this is the devil of it, that a man is not only killed, but made to look so vile and filthy in death, so futile and meaningless that you hate the sight of him.[20]

No one could see glory in such deaths. Yet what could the horrific entry in a private diary do to help others understand? When West wrote such words it was with no expectation that they would be read by anyone but himself. They were a statement of fact, an attempt to write all the terrible details out of his system. It was for the poets to translate such facts into words the world could understand. Thus, Sassoon in 'Counter Attack' takes up a similar theme:

> The place was rotten with dead; green clumsy legs
> High-booted, sprawled and grovelled along the saps,
> And trunks, face downwards, in the sucking mud,
> Wallowed like trodden sandbags loosely filled;
> And naked sodden buttocks, mats of hair,
> Bulged, clotted heads slept in the plastering slime.

The description is offensive and is meant to be, for death in such a fashion is an offence against human dignity. For all too many of those dead soldiers not even a cross marked their burial place, and if death was an end to their suffering Sassoon did not intend his readers to see suffering as ended. It is re-enacted in the poem, just as it is in Rosenberg's poem, 'Dead Man's Dump':

> The wheels lurched over sprawled dead
> But pained them not, though their bones crunched,
> Their shut mouths made no moan. . . .
> Burnt black by strange decay
> Their sinister faces lie,
> The lid over each eye.

It is clearly important to the poet that his reader should have no excuse for seeing any nobility in such deaths; the active lurch of the wheels chimes with the crunch of the bones, but the dead themselves are inactive, unmoved; they are sprawled, their mouths are shut their voices silent, their eyes unseeing. Yet one is inescapably in the presence of physical suffering; the ungainly corpses are treated without care or reverence, not only because in the presence of so many dead the soldiers have lost their respect for life, but also because it was impossible, given the circumstances of trench warfare, to do more at that moment than '[leave these] dead with the older dead,/Stretched at the cross roads'. Even this last view of the dead is symbolic of sacrifice with its Crucifixion image, though Rosenberg himself was a Jew.

Insensibility towards the dead is a theme presented by Arthur Graeme West not only in his diary, but also in his poetry. In 'Night Patrol' the horror of the battlefield was intensified by the stench from the corpses lying everywhere, yet to the soldiers on patrol each dead man was a landmark to help them back to their own trenches:

> Only the dead were always present—present
> As a vile sickly smell of rottenness;
> The rustling stubble and the early grass,
> The slimy pools—the dead men stank through all,
> Pungent and sharp; as bodies loomed before,
> And as we passed, they stank: then dulled away
> To that vague foetor, all encompassing,
> Infecting earth and air. They lay, all clothed,
> Each in some new and piteous attitude
> That we well marked to guide us back.[21]

Despite the actualities of war the occasional romantic tried to retain the romance, the spirit of careless courage which the soldiers of 1914 carried into battle. In his poetic evocation of 'Third Ypres' Edmund Blunden deflated this spirit, for death came first to such men and, even for them, death in war is shown as repulsively ugly:

> And you,
> Poor signaller, you I passed by this emplacement,
> You whom I warned, poor daredevil, waving your flags,
> Among this screeching I pass you again and shudder
> At the lean green flies upon the red flesh madding.[22]

Such then was the first, and the most straightforward, of the tasks of the realist poets; to depict the truth about the physical horrors of war. On this at least, every soldier who had seen trench warfare was agreed, and this kind of result of battle was visible before their eyes. Had physical discomfort and suffering been all that the poets wished to convey, however, the tale could soon have been told. Poet and reader alike would soon reach satiety. What emerges most clearly from the realist war poetry is the mental, moral and spiritual dilemma of the men who were fighting.

·CHAPTER·FOUR·

1

Greater love hath no man than this, that a man lay down his life for his friends.

WHEN IT WAS SEEN that the romance of war had been an illusion, when the glory of war was being reckoned in death and human suffering, when the would-be heroes were seen to be victims, then there was a great wave of compassion for all victims. In the minds of men fighting in France the world was divided into two—the safe and the suffering. The safe were all the people at home and all those in the army with 'cushy' jobs. The suffering were the men and officers in the trenches on both sides of the line.

Once in France a soldier was completely isolated from ordinary life. In the first place he was living wholly among men. The chores which were normally done for him by his womenfolk were done by other men: his food was prepared by men; his personal washing he did himself, or if he were an officer it was done by his batman. Once in the Line he saw no women at all. Further back behind the lines the only women who remained in the war area were the prostitutes living in the brothels and the occasional innkeeper's wife making her fortune by cheating the army for their drinks. Secondly, he was, in most instances, wholly engaged in death and destruction. Whereas in England he would have been working steadily at a job, however monotonous, building up his home, living with his family and playing with his children, in France his body and mind were directed towards destroying everything that he and others had previously thought worthwhile. Finally, his whole mode of life was at variance with normal life. He lived, ate, slept, suffered and often died in the same place. His home for much of the time was a hole in the ground which he shared with others whose lives were centred there.

It is not surprising that wholly artificial attitudes to many aspects of life prevailed, for life itself was unreal. Its usual ordered daily round was completely disrupted and a new, though temporary, order was necessary to save it from chaos. Those who clung too tenaciously to their old life found that the mental and spiritual upheaval was too great to be contained. Writing to the Master of Marlborough on the first anniversary of the outbreak of war Charles Sorley ended his letter with the words, 'A year ago to-day—but that way madness lies.' Thus, the acceptance of a new mode of life was as essential to the survival of the whole man as were the physical safety precautions in the dugouts.

One would perhaps expect friction among men living under such conditions, but there is rarely any mention of friction in the writings of the period. There was, on the other hand, a strong sense of comradeship which frequently appeared to develop into love. This was scarcely surprising: the attention, the consideration, the loving care which a man would normally expect to lavish on his wife and family had in the trenches to be devoted to other men; the sick, the wounded, the dying, the fearful and the pitiful were all men, tended by other men, their comrades; their trust and reliance on each other had to be absolute; their lives were in each other's hands. Such are the conditions which breed the beginnings of love, and it is quite clear that some sort of idealistic homosexuality flourished in the trenches.

In contrast to his own life of misery, discomfort and toil the soldier began to see life at home in England as comfortable, careless, self-indulgent, and the representatives of life at home were those who could never be identified with the soldier-victims. The children growing up were themselves potential victims, neither responsible for, nor desirous of sending men to France. But the older generation and the women (justly or not) could not be identified with the soldiers' suffering and thus could have no part in the life of the men in France. To measure the love of one man for one woman against the universal compassion for all those who were victims was scarcely worthwhile: romantic love between the sexes was weighed in the balance and found wanting. This is not, of course, to say that once in France the English soldier became in any way actively homosexual. Physical love between a soldier and the object of his love at home in England was denied to him; physical lust could be fulfilled in the brothels, but true spiritual love lived and flourished between man

73

and man in the trenches and was as real and poignant as is the love of a man for a woman:

> at present the only form of beauty which thrills me at all is the beauty of strong limbs and the beauty of the human expression. I am even so limited as not to care for female beauty, but only for the male! A graceful boy with the wonderful smile of youth, or a strong man with a look of resolution and compassion fill me with pleasure.[1]

Time was against romantic love between man and woman. In the present, which had to be lived and endured, it was necessary for men to love and care for each other. John Buchan, in his memoir of Francis and Riversdale Grenfell, wrote of the 'intimate ties' which bind together the members of a regiment, and described Francis's 'aching affection for his regiment' as 'the devotion of "a lover or a child"'.[2] Ten years after the war had ended Edmund Blunden recalled simply this 'aching affection' that many officers must have felt for their men:

> Daniels, Davey, Ashford, Roberts, Worley, Clifford, Seall, Unstead, do you remember me yet? I should know you among ten thousand. Your voices are heard, and each man longed for, beyond the maze of mutability.[3]

The warmth of affection, the longing, and the belief in the immutability of love are reminiscent of romantic love, but are offered to the memory of Blunden's men. There was no embarrassment in the expression of such love; it was described in letters home and it was written down in men's personal diaries. A few days before his death in action J. S. Engall wrote to his parents telling them that next day he would be leading an assault against the Germans, taking with him the 'men whom I have got to love, and who, I think, have got to love me'.[4] And Ralph Scott, using terms of endearment which are exchanged between lovers, wrote in his diary for the 18th of August 1918 of 'these dear, darling fellows of mine'.

Over and over again one reads of love and affection between the fighting men and of devotion beyond the bounds of ordinary comradeship: men giving their lives to save their officers or their comrades, officers sacrificing themselves for the sake of men under them. Just as poetry has been the vehicle for romantic love throughout the ages, so the strong emotional bond between soldier and soldier found expression in poetry of one kind or another. The sentimental songs of romance were paralleled by the rather banal verses which were published in the Trench magazines, such as the lines from *The Somme-Times* for 31 July 1916:

> But we've also learnt, and 'tis good to know,
> That the pal of a dug-out's a friend worth-while,
> For friendship made 'neath the star-shell's glow
> Means 'Help every lame dog over a stile.'[5]

Sydney Oswald, a Major in the King's Royal Rifle Corps, wrote in 'The Dead Soldier' of the love between two soldiers, one of whom had been killed in battle. His choice of 'eyes ... lips ... mouth ... heart' suggests some affinities with Wilfred Owen's poem 'Greater Love' and it is quite possible that Owen read Oswald's poem for it was published in the Trench edition of *Soldier Poets* in September 1916 and we know that Owen owned a copy of this book:

> Thy dear brown eyes which were as depths where truth
>   Lay bowered with frolic joy, but yesterday
> Shone with the fire of thy so guileless youth,
>   Now ruthless death has dimmed and closed for aye.
>
> Those sweet red lips, that never knew the stain
>   Of angry words or harsh, or thoughts unclean,
> Have sung their last gay song. Never again
>   Shall I the harvest of their laughter glean.
>
> The goodly harvest of thy laughing mouth
>   Is garnered in; and lo! the golden grain
> Of all thy generous thoughts, which knew no drouth
>   Or meanness, and thy tender words remain
>
> Stored in my heart; and though I may not see
>   Thy peerless form nor hear thy voice again,
> The memory lives of what thou wast to me.
>   We knew great love.... We have not lived in vain*.

---

*It has been suggested above that Owen may well have read 'The Dead Soldier' before writing 'Greater Love' which treats of a love more spiritual, more sacrificial than the 'great love' of Oswald's last line. Though slightly digressionary here it may be remarked that the poem facing 'The Dead Soldier' in *Soldier Poets* is also by Sydney Oswald and is entitled 'Dulce et Decorum est pro Patria Mori', a theme which Owen discredited once and for all in a poem which could well be an answer to Oswald's.

It is an over-sentimentalized poem, full of irritating poeticisms—the use of the archaic second person singular, the occasional inversion of noun and epithet to suit rhyme or rhythm, the 'poetic' vocabulary that depends on sound, not meaning. Its interest here, however, is that Oswald had no hesitation in writing in conventional romantic love terms of a man, and that at the time his sentiments were not thought of as strange or unusual; the verses were accepted for publication and published in a book which had wide distribution among the fighting men; there was no outcry against such apparently unnatural love for, in fact, the sentiments were common to many men.

A more realistic and more forceful potrayal of love between men was made by the few real poets of the war. Robert Graves gave firm expression to the bond which grew up between men in his poem 'Two Fusiliers':

> there's no need of pledge or oath
> To bind our lovely friendship fast,
> By firmer stuff
> Close bound enough.
>
> By wire and wood and stake we're bound,
> By Fricourt and by Festubert,
> By whipping rain, by the sun's glare,
> By all the misery and loud sound,
> By a Spring day,
> By Picard clay.
>
> Show me the two so closely bound
> As we, by the wet bond of blood,
> By friendship, blossoming from mud,
> By Death.[6]

As in the poetry of romantic love the imagery is taken from the minutiae of the joint life of the two men: the barriers set up in No Man's Land, the French villages, the mud, the blood pouring from wounds. At the same time there is a faint suggestion in the first line quoted of the rejection of romantic love: lover's tokens and oaths of constancy are not necessary, since the bonds forged by war are binding enough.

Like Graves, Sir Herbert Read used the love between two men to show the sort of love and affection engendered in the trenches. Typical of his method of presentation, he particularised with an actual incident:

> '*O beautiful men, O men I loved*
> *O whither are you gone, my company*'. . . .
> *A man of mine*
>   *lies on the wire;*
> *And he will rot*
> *and first his lips*
> *the worms will eat.*
> *It is not thus I would have him kiss'd*
> *but with the warm passionate lips*
> *of his comrade here.*

In these lines the savage picture narrows down to a concentration on
the lips, a focal point for the imaginations of romantic love, and the
poet is now ready to use the romantic terms 'kissed' and 'warm
passionate', not for conventional love, but for delineating the love
between an officer and one of his men.

Most writers, however, display a much more general love between
comrades than is shown in the poems of Graves and Read quoted
above. Ivor Gurney enlarged his sympathies in 'Recompense' to
embrace his friendship with all the men of the 2/5 Gloucester Regi-
ment:

> *I'd not have missed one single scrap of pain*
> *That brought me to such friends, and them to me;*
> *And precious is the smallest agony,*
> *The greatest, willingly to bear again—*
> *Cruel frost, night vigils, death so often ta'en*
> *By Golgothas untold from Somme to Sea.*
>
> *   *   *
>
> *Their eyes were stars within the blackest night*
> *Of Evil's trial. Never mariner*
> *Did trust so in the ever-fixed star*
> *As I in those.*[7]

The biblical reference to Golgotha and the use of the word 'agony'
so closely associated with the death of Christ, enrich and intensify
the ideas of friendship and love which he expresses. Yet the Christian
reference is followed by a metaphor taken from the literature of
romantic love and used to describe the men he loved. For Siegfried
Sassoon love manifested itself in an aching longing for all those who
shared the misery of war, and separation from them, though not of
his own choosing, brought out an agony of love, regret and guilt.
Again he tried through his poetry to voice feelings common to many

soldiers and to resolve the moral and spiritual dilemma they felt when at home on leave or wounded—the simultaneous desire to escape from further physical torture and to return to it in order not to appear to be deserting their comrades. His poem, 'Banishment', may well remind us of the central act of *Romeo and Juliet* in which first Juliet and then Romeo bewail his banishment. The allusion is relevant, for Sassoon saw himself as avoiding death by being banished from the trenches and yet preferring the risk of death. However, the romantic moanings of Romeo that 'heaven is here/Where Juliet lives' are strangely twisted by Sassoon, for his love for his fellows demands a return to hell:

> *I am banished from the patient men who fight*
> *They smote my heart to pity, built my pride.*
>
> *   *   *
>
> *The darkness tells how vainly I have striven*
> *To free them from the pit where they must dwell*
> *In outcast gloom convulsed and jagged and riven*
> *By grappling guns. Love drove me to rebel.*
> *Love drives me back to grope with them through hell.*[8]

So far the poems which I have quoted illustrate how love flourished in the trenches between man and man. It is clearly only a step further to the symbolic rejection of romantic love between man and woman. In the face of the stark realities of war romantic love appeared to be irrelevant, unable to measure up to the demands of life as it was being lived, not false, but not wholly true as it could not encompass the whole truth. Wilfred Owen in 'Apologia Pro Poemate Meo' took up an imagery similar to that used by Graves in 'Two Fusiliers', but he added a dimension of bitterness by a contrast with romantic presentation:

> *I have made fellowships—*
> *Untold of happy lovers in old song.*
> *For love is not the binding of fair lips*
> *With the soft silk of eyes that look and long,*
>
> *By Joy, whose ribbon slips,—*
> *But wound with war's hard wire whose stakes are strong;*
> *Bound with the bandage of the arm that drips;*
> *Knit in the webbing of the rifle-thong.*

The lines are deliberately anti-romantic: love in the context of sexual desire—'the binding of fair lips', 'the soft silk of eyes that look and long'—is insufficient, since it fails in the human situation which the soldiers in the trenches faced. The old songs may tell of bonds between happy lovers, but true love and fellowship is that which persists in misery too. It was this revelation which moved Robert Nichols in his poem 'Fulfilment', in which the fulfilment he finds is not heterosexual love and procreation, but the complete abandonment of all his thoughts and feelings and his whole being to love for his comrades and fellow-victims in war:

> *Was there love once? I have forgotten her.*
> *Was there grief once? grief yet is mine.*
> *Other loves I have, men rough, but men who stir*
> *More grief, more joy, than love of thee and thine.*

> *Faces cheerful, full of whimsical mirth,*
> *Lined by the wind, burned by the sun;*
> *Bodies enraptured by the abounding earth,*
> *As whose children we are brethren: one.*

> *   *   *

> *Was there love once? I have forgotten her.*
> *Was their grief once? grief yet is mine.*
> *O loved, living, dying, heroic soldier,*
> *All, all, my joy, my grief, my love, are thine!*[9]

Love for a woman cannot be sustained in the great and overwhelming need to focus all the tender emotions of love and solicitude upon the men who are his comrades. Nichols is striving towards the expression of an attitude which finds its poetic culmination in Wilfred Owen's 'Greater Love':

> *Red lips are not so red*
> *As the stained stones kissed by the English dead.*
> *Kindness of wooed and wooer*
> *Seems shame to their love pure.*
> *O Love, your eyes lose lure*
> *When I behold eyes blinded in my stead!*

Your slender attitude
Trembles not exquisite like limbs knife-skewed,
Rolling and rolling there
Where God seems not to care;
Till the fierce love they bear
Cramps them in death's extreme decrepitude.

Your voice sings not so soft,—
Though even as wind murmuring through raftered loft,—
Your dear voice is not dear,
Gentle, and evening clear,
As theirs whom none now hear,
Now earth has stopped their piteous mouths that coughed.

Heart, you were never hot,
Nor large, nor full like hearts made great with shot;
And though your hand be pale,
Paler are all which trail
Your cross through flame and hail:
Weep, you may weep, for you may touch them not.

Owen laid great emphasis upon the perfection or completeness of experience: emotions that were not sufficient for all human experience lacked ultimate truth—hence, romantic love was deficient, but the love by which a man laid down his life for others was perfect and holy, and the poem identifies it with the love of Jesus, also a victim, Who lay down His life for others. The poem is made effective by the cumulative power of the comparisons throughout; the inadequacy of romantic love is emphasized by the repeated negatives which open each stanza, whilst the sacrificial aspect of the Christ-like love of the soldiers is emphasized by the religious references, leading us in the last stanza through the Crucifixion to the moment of the Resurrection: 'Mary stood without the sepulchre weeping . . . Jesus saith unto her, "Touch me not"' (St. John, XX. 11–17). Here we are able to see the poet transcending the sentiment which gave rise to his poem and sublimating the experience of love.

Professor Joseph Cohen has developed and documented a phrase from the American re-issue of Robert Graves's *Goodbye To All That*, which describes Owen as 'an idealistic homosexual with a religious background'.[10] Discussing the usual pattern of homosexuality Cohen comes to the conclusion that this pattern is clearly observable in Owen's life. There is no doubt that his documentation is correct though somewhat exaggerated. It also seems probable that much of what he says could have applied to many other men of the time and, with the documentation accomplished, and with the addition of the word 'idealistic' to 'homosexual' there seems to be no proof of Owen's proclivity, one way or the other. At the same time, Owen's religious upbringing, his dedication to his poetry (to some extent necessitated by his life and background), his flirtation with religion in his Dunsden period, and the advent of war during his early manhood, partly precluded the probability of any sustained or active heterosexual love affairs. All this, taken together with the fact of the universality of the tendency towards homosexual love among the soldiers in France, suggests that Cohen has overstated his case and has failed to qualify his diagnosis by direct reference to the circumstances surrounding it. This is not to deny that Owen was an 'idealistic homosexual', but to suggest that Professor Cohen's thesis is to some extent invalidated by the fact that the peculiar circumstances in which Owen and others found themselves during the years 1914–18 resulted in a widespread tendency towards homosexuality and that this was a phenomenon of trench warfare, idealistic because the love engendered was pure, sacrificial and untarnished by any thought or intention of carnal fulfilment.

In his *Textbook of Psycho-Sexual Disorders* Clifford Allen lists among twelve common types of homosexuality: 'Deprivation homosexuality' and explains that 'this is common in . . . situations when men are deprived of women'.[11] A few pages later he comments, 'There is considerable homosexuality in the armed forces. . . . No doubt the Service life with its frequent isolation from home and women, tends to produce isolation homosexuality'.[12] It is clear that if these statements apply under ordinary circumstances to the armed forces, they are even more relevant to the conditions of trench warfare. It should also be remembered that many of the soldiers in the trenches were still very immature, being in their late 'teens' and early twenties and that at this age many young people are both hetero-and homosexually inclined. Yet another reason for the apparent lack of physical fulfilment of homosexual inclinations can be found in the idealism that pertains to this age-group.

As a final literary support to this contention let us observe the very strongly worded statement by Richard Aldington in his 'Prologue' to *Death of a Hero*:

> Friendships between soldiers during the war were a real and beautiful and unique relationship which has now entirely vanished, at least from

Western Europe. Let me at once disabuse the eager-eyed Sodomites among my readers by stating emphatically once and for all that there was nothing sodomitical in these friendships. I have lived and slept for months, indeed years, with 'the troops', and had several such companionships. But no vaguest proposal was ever made to me; I never saw any sign of sodomy, and never heard anything to make me suppose it existed. However, I was with the fighting troops. I can't answer for what went on behind the lines.

No, no. There was no sodomy about it. It was just a human relationship, a comradeship, an undemonstrative exchange of sympathies between ordinary men racked to extremity under a great common strain in a great common danger.[13]

2

'Who is my neighbour?'

THE LOVING COMRADESHIP which existed between soldiers in the trenches was based on a sympathetic identification with each other's lot. *All* were victims, unable to help themselves, compelled to wait and suffer until they were released by death or mutilation. At first sight it would appear that the German soldiers in the opposite line were responsible for inflicting all the agonies upon them. This view was soon discredited, however, and fellow-feeling was extended to the German soldiers. They too were victims, under the same compulsions as the Allied soldiers. As early in the war as the 15th of September 1914 a correspondent to *The Times* quoted in his report the remarks made to him by a French soldier:

[The Germans] are our enemies but they are also men. And see, there are women who wait for them, and children who prattle of their homecoming.

Such an attitude, so early in the war, was, in fact, not very typical. To begin with most men hated, or thought they hated, the enemy soldiers. It was not until they came face to face with them and saw the predicament of all soldiers in the trenches as being the same, that the hatred abated. There is an interesting letter from Julian Grenfell to his parents in which one can see this very process of change of heart:

We took a German Officer and some men prisoners in a wood the other day. One felt hatred for them as one thought of our dead; and as the Officer came by me, I scowled at him, and the men were cursing him. The Officer looked me in the face and saluted me as he passed; and I have never seen a man look so proud and resolute and smart and confident, in his hour of bitterness. It made me feel terribly ashamed of myself.[14]

Christmas Day 1914 appears to have marked a turning point in the soldiers' attitude towards the Germans. Two entries a fortnight apart in the unpublished War Diary of Harry Byett, a hospital orderly, illustrate this very well. A week before Christmas a German patient was brought into the field hospital where Byett was working. He was not popular with the wounded British soldiers, many of whom suggested they would like to finish him off. Byett concluded that there was real hatred felt by the British Tommies against their German counterparts. However, during the Christmas season a sympathetic friendship grew up between the allied soldiers and the Germans in the trenches opposite them and on the 2nd of January 1915 Byett made quite a different sort of comment in his diary:

many of the new patients tell how on Xmas Day many of the Germans came over to the Trenches, shook hands with our men, and exchanged cigarettes and cigars, and many of them vowed they would not fire another shot on ours after that.

The experience of that first wartime Christmas seems to have been common. The 'season of goodwill' meant enough to most men to make them view with distaste acts of violence and murder on Christ's nativity. All the habits of their youth directed them towards celebration at that time of the year—love, good-fellowship and merry-making. They needed little encouragement; a few brave or foolhardy men called out the message of peace, 'Merry Christmas, Jerry', to be answered by 'Merry Christmas, Tommy' from the German side. Immediately discipline was pushed aside as men from both sides jumped up on the parapets to talk, to swap cigarettes and to exchange food and drink. D. H. Bell told in his diary how there was an exchange of the dead and both sides helped to bury them. In *Old Soldiers Never Die* Frank Richards described the Christmas scenes of fraternization, beginning with written messages of Christmas greetings stuck up on boards above the Front Line parapets, and ending with the direct confrontation of hand-shaking and general merriment.[15]

All along the Front Line such scenes were common; observing them Philip Gibbs wrote in *The Soul of the War* that

> The war had become the most tragic farce in the world. The frightful senselessness of it was apparent when the enemies of two nations fighting to the death stood in the grey mist together and liked each other. They did not want to kill each other, these Saxons of the same race and blood, so like each other in physical appearance, and with the same human qualities.[16]

It was the beginning of a changed attitude towards the 'enemy'. As the war progressed the English soldiers were less and less inclined to hate their German counterparts, more and more inclined to see them as fellow-victims; as Donald Hankey wrote in *A Student in Arms*:

> the Cockney warrior does not hate the Hun. Often and often you will hear him tell his mate that 'the Bosches is just like us, they wants to get 'ome as much as we do; but they can't 'elp theirselves.'[17]

In a letter he wrote to the Canon of Canterbury on the 31st of December 1915 Ben Keeling confirmed this attitude. Declaring that few English soldiers really hated their enemies, he expressed a fellow-feeling for the German soldiers during bombardments and asserted that this made him no worse a soldier.[18] From the many similar comments made in letters home there can be no doubt that there was little genuine hatred between the opposing soldiers; on the contrary, there often seemed to be mutual sympathies between them. Arthur Graeme West writing to a friend commented:

> For the Hun I feel nothing but a spirit of amiable fraternity that the poor man has to sit just like us and do all the horrible and useless things that we do when he might be at home with his wife or his books, as he preferred.[19]

And a young journalist, second Lieutenant A. R. Williams, saw the war as a tragedy for both British and German soldiers, noting that by October 1916 it was the exception rather that the rule to find any ill-feeling against the enemy soldiers; pity for them was a more common emotion.[20] The connecting link between all these accounts and reports was the sympathy felt for those in the same predicament.

The British soldier and the German soldier were seen as essentially the same. C. E. Montague expressed this belief quite clearly in *Disenchantment*:

> While these men fought on, year after year, they had mostly been growing more void of mere spite all the time. feeling always more and more sure that the average German was just a decent poor devil like everyone else.[21]

It is quite clear that as this belief grew it added to the mental distress of the men in the trenches. If British and German soldiers were alike victims, who then was the enemy? Against whom should their hate be directed? After less than a year of war Philip Gibbs expressed the doubts of many of his fellow-countrymen when he wrote of the German soldiers:

> They had obeyed orders, they had marched to the hymn of the Fatherland, they believed, as we did, in the righteousness of their cause. But like the dead bodies of the Frenchmen and the Englishmen who lay quite close, they had been done to death by the villainy of statecraft and statesmen, playing one race against another.[22]

It was too soon for such sentiments to be universal. Gibbs's book, *The Soul of the War*, first published in 1915 was a scathing indictment of war and of those who allowed war; but by those who had any influence his words were hardly heeded. As the war dragged on, however, more and more men began to share Gibbs's doubts and to extend them, for if, after all the German soldiers were not the true enemy, what was the war about? Two months before the war was to end Ralph Scott confided this anxiety to his own diary, commenting that 'we have seen brave Germans die with faith as great as ours, and, knowing their intelligence to be not less, we must at least doubt the validity of our first conclusions'.[23] It was a distressing and soul-destroying thought to come to a soldier after more than four years of destructive war.

It is in the poetry of the realists that such ideas are explored and developed. Through a simple incident—the taking captive of a German officer—Herbert Read illustrated that the Germans were ordinary men with private lives, were in fact like their British counterparts:

Before we reached our wire
he told me he had a wife and three children
In the dug-out we gave him a whiskey. . . .

In broken French we discussed
Beethoven, Nietzsche and the International.

He was a professor
Living at Spandau
And not too intelligible.[24]

Arthur Graeme West, in a bitter poem criticizing those who wrote romantically of war, claimed that soldiers were banded together 'to maim and kill their fellow men'. He then added, 'For even Huns are men,'[25] a stark and simple reminder, but one which places the Germans on a more sympathetic footing than the 'young cheerful men/Whose pious poetry blossoms'.[25] W. N. Ewer's poem 'Five Souls' has close affinities with the words of Ralph Scott quoted above. In this poem five souls of men from different nations and backgrounds talk about their contribution to the war. The sting of the poem comes in the five-times repeated chorus which ends each stanza:

Third Soul

I worked in Lyons at my weaver's loom,
When suddenly the Prussian despot hurled
His felon blow at France and at the world;
Then I went forth to Belgium and my doom.
I gave my life for freedom—This I know
For those who bade me fight had told me so.

Fourth Soul

I owned a vineyard by the wooded Main
Until the Fatherland, begirt by foes
Lusting her downfall, called me, and I rose
Swift to the call—and died in far Lorraine.
I gave my life for freedom—This I know
For those who bade me fight had told me so.

Fifth Soul

I worked in a great shipyard by the Clyde;
There came a sudden word of wars declared,
Of Belgium, peaceful, helpless, unprepared,
Asking our aid: I joined the ranks, and died.
I gave my life for freedom—This I know
For those who bade me fight had told me so.[26]

The thought that most appeared to move the poets was the futility of hate towards the German soldiers. Not only were the Germans men, like those opposing them, but, when all had been said and done, the suffering and death on both sides, indeed the whole war, would appear fruitless, a backward step for mankind. It was an idea that the world at large was not ready for (is perhaps still not ready for), but it was an idea that had taken clear hold of thousands of men directly participating in the futility. The visionary and religious quality of this idea is made apparent by the constant theme of reconciliation through death and in some after life. On earth, in war, reconciliation was impossible: the Christmas truces with their Christian love and fellowship broke down when Christmas was over. Only the dead could be eternally reconciled. In 'Enemies' Siegfried Sassoon shows one such reconciliation taking place:

> He stood alone in some queer sunless place
> Where Armageddon ends. Perhaps he longed
> For days he might have lived; but his young face
> Gazed forth untroubled: and suddenly there thronged
> Round him the hulking Germans that I shot
> When for his death my brooding rage was hot.
>
> He stared at them half-wondering; and then
> They told him how I'd killed them for his sake—
> Those patient, stupid, sullen ghosts of men;
> And still there seemed no answer he could make.
> At last he turned and smiled. One took his hand
> Because his face could make them understand.

For the soldier involved in battle and destruction understanding seemed impossible in life and Armageddon could end only in death. Yet Sassoon's poem, bereft of his habitual irony, only partially achieves the sense of compassion and universal love he appears to be grasping for. The ending is weak and not very convincing.

It is once more in a poem of Owen's that this idea is perfected. 'Strange Meeting' was described by Blunden in his edition of Owen's poems as an 'Unfinished poem', but though the manuscript had clearly not been finalized the poem is, to all intents and purposes finished and perfect of its kind. It brings out the agonizing hopelessness and futility of war in which two men of differing nations, but of similar outlook can fight and kill each other, destroy the beauty and truth of life and, though men of foresight and vision, set back the hopes of mankind. The poem lays great emphasis on the idea of truth and the truth it demonstrates is 'The pity of war, the pity war distilled'. It is a poem which does not offer much hope for unlike Sassoon's vision, it does not attain to ultimate reconciliation after death; for this, both nations have to wait for peace.

3

Perhaps the French saying is true:
'It is not a tragedy to grow old, the tragedy is not to grow old.'

AS THE WAR PROGRESSED the apparent hate between the combatants turned easily to love and to a sympathetic identification. Those involved in the bestialities of war began to feel only pity for others so involved. Those who held on to hate were the people at home who could have no possible self-identification with the lives of the soldiers in the trenches. Alan Seeger, who at the outset of the war had expressed such joy at the possibility of adventure offered to him,[27] asserted in an article published in New York in *The Sun* on the 28th of April 1915 that the 'hymns of hate, the rancour and vindictiveness are the expressions of non-combatants whose venom has time to accrue in the quiet of studies far from the noise of the cannon'. The fact that the soldiers on opposing sides in the trenches had more in common with each other than with the people of their own nation back at home made it fairly certain that resentment and bitterness would arise. The pleasures and luxuries of life in England were a clear target for attack; one officer wrote to *The Times* on the 17th of November 1914 that a law should forbid a football being kicked. This was followed up in the same paper a week later, by a letter from another officer who claimed:

> I tell you this war is the most appalling crime that was ever committed, and if only English people, living in their unharmed luxury at home, could catch a glimpse of the utter misery that exists where fighting is and has been, they would be absolutely horrified.[28]

Later in the war George Sherston (alias Siegfried Sassoon), stationed back in England recuperating from an illness, visited the Olympic

88

Hotel, Liverpool, for a meal and observed the opulence and self-indulgence of a number of non-combatants 'doing themselves pretty well out of the war'.[29] Their Lucullian feast sickened Sherston as he thought of the deprivations his comrades in France were suffering. That his experience was by no means unique is well illustrated by an article on restaurants and food in London which appeared in *The Times* for the 21st of June 1916, ten days before the Battle of the Somme began. The article contained considerable discussion of what foods were available in many of the luxury restaurants and a number of menus were quoted:

At one restaurant [in Soho] where hundreds of people dine every night the following bill of fare was placed last night before the patrons:—

Hors d'oeuvre, choice of two soups, choice of braised beef with asparagus tops, escallopes of sweetbreads and peas, or bouchée à la Reine, Punch à la Romaine, chicken and salad, Neapolitan ices, cheese, and dessert.

What is fitting in [the case of soldiers on leave] is only irritating in the case of civilians, who are making money out of the war and spending it carelessly and in the pursuit of pleasure . . . with many of them their only excuse would appear to be that they have nothing else to do.

An equally straight report had appeared in *The Times* six months earlier on the 3rd of January; this was a report on 'War Prosperity' in Sheffield:

'Munitions' has come to be a magic word among the workers of Sheffield. . . .

The weekly outpourings of money in wages has swollen to a remarkable total . . . Wives who have long wished for a sideboard, or a sewing-machine, or some other article which in ordinary times has been beyond their means, are at last able to realize their ambitions. . . .

Young mechanics are buying motor-cycles, often with a sidecar attached . . . Women . . . are now considering costumes costing £4 and even £5, guinea hats, and expensive shoes. . . .

Jewellers are doing an extensive business in rings, gold bracelets, brooches, lockets, and other trinkets . . .

The Christmas holiday gave men the first real break in their labour for many months. Most of the shops were shut down for three days, and an attempt to start again last Tuesday was not altogether successful. . . . Munition workers . . . found rest so attractive that many did not resume on Tuesday.

Kipling, after 1915 vicariously involved in the struggle through the death of his son, commented on such holidays in a brief but bitter epigram:

> *If any mourn us in the workshop, say*
> *We died because the shift kept holiday.*[30]

When men came home on leave from the trenches it was the shock of this sort of contrast that met them: soldiers living meagrely, ill-fed, ill-clothed, in constant danger, and at home men and women enjoying better standards of living than normal. While they were in the trenches men longed for leave to escape their physical wretchedness, their fear and their misery, but at home they were unable to settle down and found themselves longing to return to France. There the soldiers were poorly fed, poorly clothed, poorly paid, but at least they were working together for a common cause, caring for each other. It made them 'fuming and sullen' as Philip Gibbs explained, to find that at home, 'Munition workers were earning wonderful wages and spending them on gramophones, pianos, furs and the "pictures". Everybody was gadding about in a state of joyous exaltation'.[31] The emotions felt towards the people at home were very mixed, but gradually some sort of hatred began to come to the fore, not hatred of individuals, but hatred of a nebulous mass who appeared to be saving their own lives at the expense of others. The following extract from a letter to his wife by Harold Chapin is typical:

I wish to God England would come into this war and get it over! I told you I thought November. It won't be November twelvemonth unless England drops attacking Kitchener, attacking the *Daily Mail*, attacking defenceless Germans in London, striking and all the rest of it, and devotes all its attention to attacking the German Army out here. . . . Every man not engaged in supplying food and warmth and order . . . should be directly engaged in supplying strength towards the ending of the war. If he isn't doing so he is contributing by neglect to that killing and maiming of our men out here *which he might be preventing*.[32]

The universal wish began to arise that people at home should be forced to understand the soldiers' predicament; the desire for them to be compelled to share the miseries and horrors of the men in the trenches grew; 'the best way to buck them up would be a hundred thousand Germans landing in England' was the comment in one letter to *The Times*, and the writer went on to say that this 'would bring home to the smug armchair brigade as nothing else will something at least of the awful way in which Belgium and part of France has suffered'.[33] Writing his recollections of the war Philip Gibbs told how soldiers became more and more bitter as time went on against those who stayed at home and enriched themselves through the suffering of others. They began, he claimed, to express the desire 'that profiteers should die by poison-gas. They prayed God to get the Germans to send Zeppelins to England—to make the people know what war meant'.[34] To prove that his remarks were true there are letters such as this one from an officer in France published in *The Times* for the 26th of October 1915:

I see from the papers that Zeppelins have dropped bombs on London again. I cannot even say that I am sorry. It is the only thing that reminds the people at home that the war is still continuing. If only they were sufficiently awake to realize one-hundredth part of what our men suffer out here, how differently they would behave!

The soldiers in France and the people at home were spiritually completely out of touch with each other. The degree of privation and of suffering differed so immeasurably that the points of contact became fewer and fewer. In England the lack of understanding of the suffering which the soldiers at the front endured was absolute because that suffering was beyond comprehension to those who had not seen it. Meanwhile the men in France condemned those at home for not understanding, for not suffering. Robert Nichols described how there seemed to be 'two England's':

individuals, returned from leave, reported a queer, hectic England . . . strangely at variance with the mood of the trenches. Leave or a wound soon assured the fighting soldier of the existence of two Englands—the England that was in the trenches and the England elsewhere—and of two wars—the war that was waged with flesh and blood and the war that was waged with words. . . . Profiteers, arrogant Brasshats in 'cushy' jobs, jacks-in-office and embusqués generally, plethoric elders full of vindictiveness and ignorant opinions, jaunty newspapers, womankind running loose, civilians labouring under the delusion that they were suffering severely because they had a meat card and no petrol.[35]

In the same category as the 'people-at-home', that is, sacrificers as opposed to victims, were the staff, the 'Brasshats' to whom Nichols refers in the quotation above. The combat officers, sharing in the dangers and miseries of the men were accepted as being on the right side, but the officers organizing manoeuvres from offices in England and the Staff comfortably billeted well behind the lines, well-shaved, wearing clean uniforms were seen in the same light as any other non-combatant. It does seem that these latter particularly were incredibly obtuse in their attitudes; not having experience of fighting at first hand they were still concerned with the usual ludicrous attention to unimportant details which bedevils armies. As Blunden explained,

The war as we saw it fell into two zones:—first, In the Trenches, but less baited and badgered by gorgeous numsculls: second, Out of the Trenches, and suffering from the official terror that we might fall into indolent habits. Thus we were between devil and deep sea.[36]

The word 'gorgeous' is especially telling, implying a material description of neat and tidy uniforms, possible only out of the fighting zone, decorations given for no one knew what, a foppish, feminine outlook to what should have been a strong and masculine experience. At the same time it implies a definite despising of those who are being described; it is not a word that a man uses of another man whom he respects. Frank Richards, who represents well the view of the ordinary soldier, affirmed that

We all hated the sight of Staff officers and the only damned thing the majority seemed to be any good at was to check men who were out of action for not saluting them properly.[37]

The attitude of the non-combatants was a theme taken up and developed by the realist poets, in particular by Owen and Sassoon, but also by lesser-known poets. Alexander Robertson wrote a poem inspired by a deliberately parodied quotation from Campbell which he used as his title, 'We shall drink to them that Sleep'.[38] Like other soldiers he was especially embittered by the thought that people at home were battening on the soldiers' lives by luxurious living. Had they lived lives of deprivation the soldiers could have seen war as touching them more nearly, but the reverse seemed to be the case, and to make the deaths of those killed in France an excuse for self-indulgence was anathema to soldiers like Robertson:

> *Yes, I can see you at it, in a room*
> *Well-lit and warm, high-roofed and soft to the tread,*
> *Satiate and briefly mindful of the tomb*
> *With its poor victim of Teutonic lead.*
>
> *Some unknown notability will rise,*
> *Ridiculously solemn, glass abrim,*
> *And say, 'To our dear brethren in the skies,'—*
> *Dim are all eyes, all glasses still more dim.*

The evocation of the trenches through an inverted description is skilfully managed; 'a room/Well-lit . . . warm, high-roofed . . . soft to the tread'—all in fact, that the trenches are not, yet all accepted unquestioningly by those met to do honour to the dead of whom they are but 'briefly mindful'. The change in the quotation of the title is significant too, for here the deaths of soldiers just provide further opportunities for celebration on the part of the non-combatants who, whilst they scarcely 'think' seriously about the dead, are only too ready to drink to them. The verses are well-contrived and not entirely without merit, though very lightweight. It was not only the versifiers and minor poets, however, who enlarged on this theme. The indulgence in luxury is also criticized by Owen in 'The Calls':

> *Gongs hum and buzz like saucepan lids at dusk,*
> *I see a food-hog whet his gold filled tusk*
> *To eat less bread, and more luxurious rusk.*

and by Sassoon in 'The Fathers':

> *Snug at the club two fathers sat,*
> *Gross, goggle-eyed and full of chat.*

In these poems the criticism of people at home is implicit in the implied contrasts with life in the trenches, where even fresh bread was a luxury, where to be 'snug' and 'gross' was unknown. There is too, a certain amount of explicit criticism; the images used by Owen, 'food-hog' and 'gold-filled tusk' are unpleasant ones, animal terms, which underline a complete lack of identification with men in the human predicament, and Sassoon's 'gross, goggle-eyed' fathers are unsympathetic figures, though perhaps pitiable rather than repulsive.

War propaganda and recruiting slogans helped to widen the gap between soldiers and civilians for they seemed to emanate from the older generation who were seen as hypocritical and completely lacking in true understanding. E. A. Mackintosh voiced the feelings of many soldiers in his lines on 'Recruiting'; they are in themselves little more than propaganda, but they point towards the bitterness which made more serious poets present the theme of the rift between those at home and those in the trenches:

> *'Lads, you're wanted, go and help',*
> *On the railway carriage wall*
> *Stuck the poster, and I thought*
> *Of the hands that penned the call.*
>
> *Fat civilians wishing they*
> *'Could go and fight the Hun.'*
> *Can't you see them thanking God*
> *That they're over forty-one?*
>
>   ***   ***   ***
>
> *Better twenty honest years*
> *Than their dull three score and ten.*
> *Lads you're wanted. Come and learn*
> *To live and die with honest men.*[39]

It was Sassoon, however, who expressed the savage hatred developed in the soldiers' wishes that the people at home should suffer the same miseries, deprivations and fears as were suffered in the trenches. Of this kind of poems his 'Blighters' is the most effective:

> *The House is crammed: tier beyond tier they grin*
> *And cackle at the Show, while prancing ranks*
> *Of harlots shrill the chorus, drunk with din;*
> *'We're sure the Kaiser loves our dear old tanks!'*
>
> *I'd like to see a Tank come down the stalls,*
> *Lurching to rag-time tunes, or 'Home, sweet Home,'*
> *And there'd be no more jokes in Music-halls*
> *To mock the riddled corpses round Bapaume.*

The scene is set up in the first stanza with the wild and careless self-indulgence of the Music-hall. The choice of vocabulary introduces value-judgments from the start of the poem. The first stanza is concerned with those at home who are getting everything they can out of war-time life, glutting themselves with pleasure; even the hall itself is 'crammed' and the chorus is 'drunk with din'; nothing is simple and natural: the laughter is grinning and cackling; 'prancing' is not dancing, but a mockery of dancing; everything suggests a lack of self-control. Yet ominous reminders of war by the use of words with battle connotations—show, ranks, shrill—lead us on to the brainless jingle of the Music-hall song and prepare us for the twist in the second stanza. The verses are turned into a war poem with the savage starkness of the monosyllabic line 'I'd like to see a Tank come down the stalls'. The poem culminates in the bitter pathos of the last two lines with their sick pun on 'jokes . . . mock . . . riddled'. Bapaume was Haig's objective on the first day of the Battle of the Somme. By the end of the day the attackers (or those who were left of them) were back in their own trenches; what they had achieved on that first day was 20,000 men killed and 40,000 wounded. Sassoon's bitterness is not surprising, nor can it be wondered at that he wished the non-combatants to experience war. The logical outcome of this wish was its extension in order to ensure its fulfilment by direct action on the part of the victims. This idea also is expressed by Sassoon in 'Fight to a Finish', a poem which envisages the triumphant return to England of soldiers who had fought and survived:

> Snapping their bayonets on to charge the mob,
> Grim Fusiliers broke ranks with glint of steel,
> At last the boys had found a cushy job.

> * * *

> I heard the Yellow-Pressmen grunt and squeal;
> And with my trusty bombers turned and went
> To clear those Junkers out of Parliament.

Other targets for hatred and bitterness were the staff and the high-ranking officers who planned campaigns but did not participate in them. Generals were especially picked out for abuse, for they were seen as having the ultimate responsibility, yet planning trench warfare on the drawing-board and not on the field. The General of Sassoon's poem of that name is seen as such a one:

> *'Good-morning; good-morning!' the General said*
> *When we met him last week on our way to the line.*
> *Now the soldiers he smiled at are most of 'em dead,*
> *And we're cursing his staff for incompetent swine.*
> *'He's a cheery old card,' grunted Harry to Jack*
> *As they slogged up to Arras with rifle and pack.*

> *   *   *

> *But he did for them both by his plan of attack.*

A. P. Herbert wrote of a contrary situation—a successful battle in which the General's plans work—yet the result for the soldiers themselves is not so very different from failure; many of them are dead and wounded, spiritually broken despite the success. The barrier between soldiers and General is shown to be insurmountable by the General's reaction to the success; he sees only the military victory and thinks of the personal honour it will bring to him:

> *So they are satisfied with our Brigade*
>   *And it remains to parcel out the bays!*
> *And we shall have the usual Thanks Parade,*
>   *The beaming General and the soapy praise.*
>
> *You will come up in your capacious car*
>   *To find your heroes sulking in the rain,*
> *To tell us how magnificent we are,*
>   *And how you hope we'll do the same again.*
>
> *And we, who knew your old abusive tongue,*
>   *Who heard you hector us a week before,*
> *We who have bled to boost you up a rung—*
>   *A K.C.B. perhaps, perhaps a Corps—*
>
> *We who must mourn those spaces in the Mess,*
>   *And somehow fill those hollows in the heart,*
> *We do not want your Sermon on Success,*
>   *Your greasy benisons on Being Smart.*[40]

The soldiers' attitude towards the non-combatant staff is summed up in a little-known poem by Julian Grenfell. It is an ironic prayer, a parody of the type of poem which romanticizes prayer to God for safety in battle:

> Fighting in mud, we turn to Thee,
>   In these dread times of battle, Lord,
> To keep us safe, if so may be,
>   From shrapnel, snipers, shell and sword.
>
> But not on us, for we are men
>   Of meaner clay, who fight in clay,
> But on the Staff, the Upper Ten,
>   Depends the issue of the Day.
>
> The Staff is working with its brains,
>   While we are sitting in the trench;
> The Staff the universe ordains
>   (Subject to Thee and General French). . . .
>
> O Lord, who mad'st all things to be,
>   And madest some things very good,
> Please keep the extra A.D.C.
>   From horrid scenes, and sight of blood.[41]

It will be apparent that many of the verses written on such themes are little more than doggerel with a strongly propagandist tone. Their rhymes and rhythms are conventional, often trite but strong because, as with nursery songs, jingling metre and obvious rhymes are memorable. Some more powerful poems such as Sassoon's 'Blighters' quoted in full above, are superficially similar. In that poem, however, Sassoon deliberately adopted the simple form in order to re-inforce the atmosphere of the scene he was evoking and the carefully chosen vocabulary gives the poem far greater effect than the mocking and rather light tone of the verses by A. P. Herbert and Julian Grenfell.

So far in this chapter we have seen how a universal compassion arose, embracing all soldiers in the trenches, of whatever nationality and how the soldier victims saw the non-combatants as sacrificers. The emotions of love and hate were directed towards objects which they would not move towards under normal living conditions. Out of these abnormally-directed emotions grew the idea of the 'generation gap' which is so glibly talked of today as a modern phenomenon. This, together with the reshaping of the Christian myth which took place during the war years, is discussed in the next chapter.

·CHAPTER·FIVE·

1

Man is by his constitution a religious animal

DURING TIMES of especial stress the thoughts of many people turn naturally to religion, and so it was during the war period. Many men prayed to God for help and release from their misery; others saw God as the hand of Fate directing their lives, redeeming and condemning as He saw fit. This latter attitude led to a re-interpretation of the Christian myth[1] in terms suited to twentieth-century warfare. Before discussing this, however, it is helpful to look briefly at the more conventional attitudes to God and religion in which God was seen in the New Testament perspective and in which the Church and Church services were accepted as part of spiritual life, even if Christian belief were rejected.

In the conditions which prevailed in France it was comforting to have some firm belief in an all-loving, all-caring God. The assurance in a difficult situation that God would protect and help enabled men to endure their miseries more readily. Major S. H. Baker, writing to his brother of his experience stranded in No Man's Land caring for his wounded servant, told how 'We both agreed out there that God would help us somehow'.[2] The fact that they survived their ordeal, and lived to write an account of it confirmed them in their belief. On the other hand, we read in the same book a letter from J. S. Engall to his parents, full of faith and trust in God:

> I took my Communion yesterday with dozens of others who are going over tomorrow; and never have I attended a more impressive service. I placed my soul and body in God's keeping, and I am going into battle

98

with His name on my lips, full of confidence and trusting implicitly in Him. I have a strong feeling that I shall come through safely; but nevertheless, should it be God's holy will to call me away, I am quite prepared to go.[3]

This letter was written on one of the last three days of June 1916; on the 1st of July he was killed. The dilemma of belief is immediately obvious: had he survived he would have believed that God had saved and protected him; as he died he was no longer receptive of belief or disbelief. It was left to others to wonder whether God had failed him, or whether God had chosen and received him. Add to this bewildering uncertainty the equally perplexing problems as to whether God was the God of the Germans too, and whether God could help men to break the precepts that upheld Him—in other words whether He could guide the bullet, put power into the bayonet thrust, when one of His commandments was 'Thou shalt not kill', and the spiritual dismay of Christian men in the trenches is readily understandable:

God and Christianity raised perplexities in the minds of simple lads desiring life and not death. They could not reconcile the Christian precepts of the chaplain with the bayoneting of Germans and the shambles of the battlefields.[4]

In *Old Soldiers Never Die* Frank Richards posited the problem clearly when he told how an

Old Soldier had been reading in a paper that our bishops and ministers had been praying for a speedy victory and also that the German clergy had been praying for the same. 'God's truth!' he exclaimed. 'That poor old Chap above must be very nearly bald-headed through scratching His poll, trying to answer the prayers of both sides.'[5]

The poets heard the prayers: indeed some of them prayed themselves, but there is a marked absence of reverent prayers and references to God from the better poets. We find among the lesser poets Evan Morgan ending a trench poem with a stanza which begins,

> *Great God, with tending hand*
> *Watch o'er our souls.*[6]

or Captain J. E. Stewart offering thanks to God for deliverance:

> *Blessed be God above*
> *For His sweet care,*
> *Who heard the prayers of those who most I love*
> *And my poor suppliance there,*
> *Who brought me forth in life and limb all whole,*
> *Who blessed my powers with His Divine repair,*
> *And gave me back my soul!*[7]

Both poems have a slightly artificial ring about them, a religiosity that has been learned, but not felt. Robert Nichols hardly does better in his memorial poem for Richard Pinsent which concludes with a somewhat agnostic kind of prayer, questioning God's existence, but at the same time taking out a spiritual insurance policy:

> *God, if Thou livest, and indeed didst send*
> *Thine only Son to be to all a Friend,*
> *Bid His dark, pitying eyes upon me bend,*
> *And His hand heal, or I must needs despair.*[8]

Probably much more typical of Trench prayers were those spontaneous utterances in time of great misery and fear, the 'impotent wild cries to God'[9] which were rarely recorded. These are, in fact, occasionally found in the poetry of the period: 'O God, send us peace!' wrote Ivor Gurney in 'De Profundis'[10] and Sassoon ended 'Attack' with 'O Jesus, make it stop!' The only sincere, wholly perfect and beautiful battle prayer dating from this period is W. N. Hodgson's 'Before Action' with its final line refrain for each stanza, 'Make me a soldier, Lord./Make me a man, O Lord./Help me to die, O Lord.'

There were, of course, other references to God. F. W. Harvey describing a dead soldier declared that 'His soul sits safe with God.'[11] Owen, voicing belief and doubt at the same time, commented of men killed in an offensive 'Some say God caught them even before they fell.'[12] There are antagonistic references too, such as Ivor Gurney's, 'The amazed heart cries angrily out on God,'[13] but most of these verge on, or belong to, the re-interpretation of the Christian myth which is discussed in the next section.

2

'Take now thy son, thine only son Isaac, whom thou lovest, and get thee into the land of Moriah; and offer him there for a burnt-offering.'

The whole history of the Christian religion from its Old Testament origins to the heart of the New Testament story itself is bound up with the idea of sacrifice, the blood offering made to God. It begins in the fourth chapter of Genesis with God rejecting Cain's offering 'of the fruit of the ground' but respecting and accepting Abel's blood offering 'of the firstlings of his flock'. The whole story of sacrifice is intricately interwoven with that of the scapegoat. Indeed, one of the four Hebrew words translated in the Authorised Version as 'flock' can mean either 'sheep' or 'goats'. The lamb used when the Passover was instituted was 'without blemish, a male of the first year . . . from the sheep, or from the goats' and it was not only a sacrifice, but also a scapegoat, for by its blood the Israelites escaped God's punishment which was executed upon 'all the first born in the land of Egypt, both man and beast.' The killing of the firstborn of the Egyptians is another strand in the complicated web of sacrifice. It is paralleled in the New Testament by Herod's massacre of the Innocents.

Although human sacrifice was never part of the religion of the Bible there are two major references to it, apart from the massacres just referred to; one in the Old Testament, the offering of Isaac by Abraham, and the second in the New Testament, paralleling the earlier one, the offering of Jesus by God the Father. The two incidents have many features in common with each other and with the Passover sacrifice: in each instance a father offers for sacrifice his first born son; in each instance the son is innocent and without blemish. However, here the similarities end, for God intervenes in the Old Testament story and Isaac is saved, whereas in the New Testament story no one intervenes and Jesus is sacrificed.

It is slightly strange that no one has seen in these biblical stories the seeds of the concept of the 'generation gap' for this is how they were seen by the soldiers of 1914–18. In fact, the whole concept which we think of as a modern idea, dating from the mid-1950s, seems to have been formulated in a new Christian myth during that era. The 'parent-child' aspect of the relationship between Abraham and Isaac, and more importantly, between God and Jesus was exploited to draw a new parallel between these biblical victims and the victims of the war. Soldiers were seen both as the sacrificial lambs and as the scapegoats, dying to save others by their blood and dying to atone for the mistakes of an older generation which had allowed chaos to overwhelm the world. Thus, Jesus the Son was accepted and loved because He was a suffering victim, whereas God the Father was rejected and often hated because he was willing to sacrifice Jesus. This willingness was no longer seen as a personal and supreme sacrifice on the part of God the Father, but as an act of harsh and selfish egoism, not Himself to atone for the world's sins, but to send another to atone for them; the sacrifice was all on the part of Jesus the Son. Emotive words in this context were those connected with the sacrificial act of the New Testament—'Golgotha', 'Calvary', 'cross', 'agony' and so on. The soldier-victims were identified with Jesus; His lot was theirs: they suffered agony, bore their crosses, frequently endured a cruel and undeserved death; the older generation and the statesmen were identified with God and the Pharisees; they believed in the need for sacrifice and by their acts enforced it, yet it seemed not to touch them personally.

(I am aware of the element of unfairness in all this discussion: I am attempting to fix the general impression which emerges from the writings of the period and to prepare for the very vivid and vital re-interpretation of the Christian myth which occurs in the poetry.)

For 2000 years it had been taught that the death of Jesus was an end of sacrifice within the Church, that God demanded nothing further of His people but that they should accept Jesus' sacrifice which week by week was celebrated in the Churches as being a 'full, perfect, and sufficient sacrifice, oblation, and satisfaction, for the sins of the whole world.' Now the ministers of the Church seemed not only unable to give a lead in upholding the principles upon which their religion was founded, but also to be denying the fullness and sufficiency of the sacrifice that had already been made. On the 10th of April 1916 *The Times* reported the Bishop of London as saying that 'what the Church has to do is to breathe the spirit of sacrifice from end to end of this country'.

Wilfred Owen, who had quoted so approvingly in a letter to his mother in May 1917 the text 'Greater love hath no man than this that a man lay down his life—for a friend', found himself almost a year later, on the 31st of March 1918, parodying another text also concerned with the laying down of life:

> God so hated the world that He gave several millions of English-begotten sons, that whosoever believeth in them should not perish, but have a comfortable life.[14]

The difference between the originals of these texts appears to lie in the implications of the wording: in the first the laying down of life is entirely voluntary; a man shows his love by laying down his life for another; the second text implies an obligatory laying down of life: God showed His love by sacrificing His Son, that is, a life other than His own.

So the symbolic sacrifice of the One is redefined: it is no longer symbolic; it is no longer a single sacrifice; Abraham insists on offering his own sacrifice; other fathers insist on offering theirs; they reject Christ's vicarious suffering for they all have sons to give: ' . . . my father was proud that I had "done the right thing"' wrote Robert Graves, describing his enlistment,[15] and fathers would not offer their pride instead of their sons:

> *Offer the Ram of Pride instead of him.*
> *But the old man would not so, but slew his son,*
> *And half the seed of Europe, one by one.*[16]

Abraham was a target for Osbert Sitwell too. Although Isaac's life is, in fact, saved in the Biblical story, emphasis was laid upon the willingness of the father to sacrifice his son; this was seen as parallel with the willingness of the fathers of the young men of 1914–18. Sitwell's Abraham is rich, flabby, pampered—and a profiteer. He takes what he can for himself from the war, and he gives by sacrificing others:

> *Consider me and all that I have done—*
> *I've fought for Britain with my might and main;*
> *I make explosives—and I gave a son.*
> *My factory, converted for the fight*
> *(I do not like to boast of what I've spent),*
> *Now manufactures gas and dynamite,*
> *Which only pays me seventy per cent.*
> *And if I had ten other sons to send*
> *I'd make them serve my country to the end.*[17]

Sassoon uses two other Old Testament stories to parallel his own times; first, the story of Abel and Cain, one fearful, loved by God but killed by his brother, the other hated and punished by God. The second story is that of King David's treachery to Uriah the Hittite whose death in battle was deliberately planned by David. It can be seen that both these stories are concerned with the deaths of young men in circumstances not of their own choosing; both, of course, belong to the pre-Christian myth, but the protagonists of both have considerable importance as preludes to the New Testament story.

For Isaac Rosenberg with his Jewish background the sacrifice of soldiers in battle was naturally seen in pre-Christian terms. Alignment with a re-interpreted Christian myth was for him spiritually impossible yet the image which he used in 'Dead Man's Dump' combined the sacrificial pyre of the Jewish Old Testament with Nebuchadnezzar's deliberate attempt to burn to death Shadrach, Meshach and Abednego:

> *What of us who, flung on the shrieking pyre,*
> *Walk, our usual thoughts untouched,*
> *Our lucky limbs as on ichor fed,*
> *Immortal seeming ever?*

It was the idea of unwilling sacrifice which was seized upon by the soldiers in France—the thought developed that they were not sacrificing themselves, but were *being* sacrificed. The idea of laying down their lives was accompanied in the minds of the soldier-victims by the idea of there being someone to perform the sacrifice who was not personally laying down his own life. The sacrificer was always older, always more powerful, always in a position of some sort of authority. Politicians were obvious targets. Ford Madox Ford, in a letter written on the 28th of July 1916 blamed Lloyd George:

The *Daily Mail* has just come in & I see that we have taken Pozières & that the Rt. Hon D[avid] L[loyd] G[eorge] still has his back to the wall & will fight to the last drop of *our* blood.

Blaming an individual, however, was too limiting, and appeared to excuse the rest. Robert Graves was more in line with the attitude of the majority of young soldiers when he squarely presented an opposition between the older and the younger generation, asserting that by mid-1916 the continuanace of the war 'seemed merely a sacrifice of the idealistic younger generation to the stupidity and self-protective alarm of the elder'.[18] A corollary to this was the belief that religion, as represented by the Church, was doing nothing to end the war and that God the Father was, at the least, not exerting Himself to save the victims of war. The words of a young lieutenant in the Suffolk Regiment bear witness to the anxiety and bewilderment that this thought engendered:

Any faith in religion I ever had is most frightfully shaken by things I've seen, and it's incredible that if God could make a 17-inch shell not explode—it seems incredible that he lets them explode.[19]

So the kind of alignment described above began to form itself in the minds of the soldiers—the older generation, men and women at home, the government, the staff, and God the Father were on one side; the younger generation, the combatant soldiers and officers and Jesus Christ the Son were on the other side; it was, in fact, a Christ-centred religion, 'pure Christianity',[20] as Owen described it, in which the emphasis was laid on the Christ-like qualities of those who were following this new religion. Even the more conventionally religious saw the strength of this alignment, as the young Canadian, Roger Livingstone, who wrote to his mother:

Do you realize that Christ was the first one to fall in the present war? . . . The very principles for which Christ gave His life are identically those principles for which Britain is today giving her life-blood. It is an old struggle, and Christ Himself was the first martyr to the cause.[21]

Richard Aldington stated the opposition between young men on one side, and old men and women on the other, quite clearly in the poem entitled 'The Blood of the Young Men', which is full of Biblical allusions:

> Blood of the young men, blood of their bodies,
> Squeezed and crushed out to purple the garments of Dives,
> Poured out to colour the lips of Magdalen,
> Magdalen who loves not, whose sins are loveless.
> O this steady drain of the weary bodies,
> This beating of hearts growing dimmer and dimmer,
> This bitter indifference of the old men,
> This exquisite indifference of women.
>
> Old men, you will grow stronger and healthier
> With broad red cheeks and clear hard eyes—
> Are not your meat and drink the choicest?
> Blood of the young, dear flesh of the young men?

The re-interpretation of the myth crystallized in the poetry and correspondence of the realist poets. In a letter to Wilfred Owen sometime in 1918 Osbert Sitwell enclosed a brief epigram 'Ill Winds' which re-enacted and up-dated the agony and death of Jesus:

Up on the Cross, in ugly agony,
The Son of Man hung dying—and the roar
Of earthquakes rent the solemn sky
Already thundering its wrath, and tore
The dead from out their tombs. . . . Then Jesus died—
But Monsieur Clemenceau is fully satisfied![22]

The scene is at one and the same time the New Testament Calvary and the France of 1918, the fearful natural horrors enacted at the moment of Christ's death and the equally fearful unnatural horrors enacted at the deaths of the many 'Christs' who were being sacrificed in France. Over it all the distant, God-like figure of Monsieur Clemenceau (then French Premier) broods, with his peculiar satisfaction at the final enactment of the tragedy.

Writing to thank Sitwell for this epigram Owen commented in his letter:

For 14 hours yesterday I was at work—teaching Christ to lift his cross by numbers, and how to adjust his crown; I attended his Supper to see that there were no complaints; and inspected his feet that they should be worthy of the nails. I see to it that he is dumb and stands at attention before his accusers. With a piece of silver I buy him every day, and with maps I make him familiar with the topography of Golgotha.[23]

The whole passage shows, as might be expected from Owen, a close acquaintance with the language of the biblical story; at the same time it has been skilfully adapted to parallel the various aspects of a soldier's life preluding and leading up to the final consummation in his death in battle. Sassoon had already developed a similar image of the Christ-soldier in 'The Redeemer' published in *The Old Huntsman and Other Poems* during the previous year:

I turned in the black ditch, loathing the storm;
A rocket fizzed and burned with blanching flare,
And lit the face of what had been a form
Floundering in mirk. He stood before me there;
I say that He was Christ; stiff in the glare,
And leaning forward from His burdening task,
Both arms supporting it; His eyes on mine
Stared from the woeful head that seemed a mask
Of mortal pain in Hell's unholy shine.

> No thorny crown, only a woollen cap
> He wore—an English soldier, white and strong,
> Who loved his time like any simple chap,
> Good days of work and sport and homely song . . .
> He faced me, reeling in his weariness,
> Shouldering his load of planks, so hard to bear.
> I say that He was Christ, who wrought to bless
> All groping things with freedom bright as air,
> And with His mercy washed and made them fair.

The parallels are less emphasized in this poem than they are in Owen's words, perhaps because the religious background of the two poets differed considerably: Owen had been brought up in a strongly religious home and had contemplated the Church as a career whereas Sassoon's background was one of conventional religion only.

Yet it was a generation brought up to be conversant with the Authorized Version of the Bible and the biblical words are part of the common heritage, certainly of all educated men. The emotional impact of the Bible was also, speaking in general terms, greater then than it is today so that words taken from the story of the Crucifixion, were in themselves powerfully emotive. It was because of this that Herbert Read in 'The Scene of War' was able in two brief lines:

> My men, my modern Christs
> your bloody agony confronts the world

to involve his reader in re-interpreting the Christian myth according to the beliefs suggested by Owen and others.

Osbert Sitwell was particularly engrossed with the story of the Crucifixion and used it in two other war-time poems. The first of these, 'Rhapsode', describes the horror of Calvary in words relevant at the same time to death in battle:

> When Christ was slowly dying on that tree—
> Hanging in agony upon that hideous Cross—
> Tortured, betrayed, and spat upon,
> Loud through the thunder and the earthquake's roar
> Rang out
> Those blessed humble words of doubt:
> 'My God! My God! why hast Thou forsaken Me?'

But to cry out in this way was seen as unheroic, and the

> Pharisees and Sadducees,
> And all were shocked—
> Pained beyond measure.
> And they said:
> 'At least he might have died like a hero
> With an oath on his lips,
> Or the refrain from a comic song—
> Or a cheerful comment of some kind.'[24]

The other of Sitwell's poems concerned with the Crucifixion shows
the old men of Jesus' time pitying not Christ the victim, but Joseph,
His father: 'Poor Joseph! How he'll feel about his son!' Christ
Himself, however, is criticized for His bitterness and discontent, and
His generosity to His persecutors is misinterpreted:

> For when they nailed him high upon the tree,
> And gave him vinegar and pierced his side,
> He asked God to forgive them—still dissatisfied![25]

There seems little doubt that an interest in the Christian myth
was fostered and encouraged by what was to Englishmen the unex-
pectedly religious aspect of the French countryside with its 'Calvaries'
and huge Catholic Churches. Soldiers from Britain were used enough
to sleepy church spires or towers in country scenes, but the huge
religious symbols dominating the French landscape were unexpected
and impressed themselves upon the imagination. It is not unusual
to find references to them in letters home, such as the comment made
by William Burgon who had observed a massive crucifix close to a
ruined church; it was, he said, 'unscathed and intact [and] over 15
feet high'.[26] The very prominence of these religious symbols began
to foster a kind of anger and bitterness in the soldiers. Religion
seemed not only futile, but a mockery. Thus, Robert Nichols in his
poem, 'Battery moving up to a New Position from Rest Camp:
Dawn,' heard a church bell boom; he imagined the priest inside the
church celebrating Mass and offered the congregation a renewed
sacrifice to celebrate:

> O people who bow down to see
> The Miracle of Calvary,
> The bitter and the glorious,
> Bow down, bow down and pray for us.

> Once more our anguished way we take
> Toward our Golgotha, to make
> For all our lovers sacrifice.
> Again the troubled bell tolls thrice.
>
> And slowly, slowly, lifted up
> Dazzles the overflowing cup.
>
> O worshipping, fond multitude,
> Remember us too, and our blood.
>
> Turn hearts to us as we go by,
> Salute those about to die,
> Plead for them, the deep bell toll:
> Their sacrifice must soon be whole.
>
> Entreat you for such hearts as break
> With the premonitory ache
> Of bodies, whose feet, hands, and side,
> Must soon be torn, pierced, crucified.[27]

The contrast which Nichols presents between the worshipping congregation performing the sacrificial rites at their church and the suffering soldiers going towards their own re-enactment of Calvary suggests the chasm between church religion and pure Christianity. Owen uses the same theme, perhaps rather more subtly, in his 'Anthem for Doomed Youth', which is a carefully worked out negation of the Mass for the Dead.

Two short poems from Owen are of especial interest in this connection. Both originated from aspects of the Roman Catholic religion in France, both have a similar theme, and both were written in four-line stanzas of iambic tetrameters. The first is inspired by the view of a shelled Calvary:

> One ever hangs where shelled roads part.
>   In this war He too lost a limb,
> But His disciples hide apart;
>   And now the Soldiers bear with Him.
>
> Near Golgotha strolls many a priest,
>   And in their faces there is pride
> That they were flesh-marked by the Beast
>   By whom the gentle Christ's denied.
>
> The scribes on all the people shove
>   And brawl allegiance to the state,
> But they who love the greater love
>   Lay down their life; they do not hate.[28]

The Christ-figure has again been compelled to re-enact His personal sacrifice, but those who profess to follow Him have abrogated their Christian responsibility in favour of what they see as a responsibility to the state, ignoring what to Owen was the essence of Christ-centred religion, Christ's words in St John XV.13: 'Greater love hath no man than this, that a man lay down his life for his friends.' The second of these two short poems, which is again quoted in full, took its origin from the view of a shelled Church in Quivières:

> So the church Christ was hit and buried
>   Under its rubbish and its rubble.
> In cellars, packed-up saints lie serried,
>   Well out of hearing of our trouble.
>
> One virgin still immaculate
>   Smiles on for war to flatter her.
> She's halo'd with an old tin hat,
>   But a piece of hell will batter her.[29]

During both the First and Second World Wars the practice in churches at risk from shelling and bombing was to pack up their art treasures, including free standing statues, and frequently, stained-glass windows, and either convey them to a place of safety or store them in the vaults. In Roman Catholic churches, however, the Crucifix which was central to the worship of the Church, and the figure of the Virgin, the necessary intercessor, were left. Owen saw this as symbolizing his new religion: Christ Himself was ready to face the horrors and destruction of war, but His followers kept out of it. It is interesting to see his ambivalent attitude towards the Virgin Mary, since to him personally the mother-figure was almost sacred, though his idea of 'pure Christianity' in no way necessitated a reverence for the mother of Christ. Thus she was left unaligned, neither suffering with Christ and the soldiers, nor hidden away with the saints, yet the final line seems to imply that she too would have to re-enact her suffering, and this time more directly.

There can be little doubt that what people like Owen were rejecting was not Christianity as such but church religion, Christianity as it was interpretated by the Bishops and priests. There is an interesting letter from Owen to his mother written from Craiglockhart on the 13th of August 1917. It is especially significant when one remembers Owen's oppressively close relationship with his mother and at the same time considers her narrowly devout and religious nature. It is indeed a criticism of much that she had appeared to stand for:

I'm overjoyed that you think of making bandages for the wounded. Leave Black Sambo ignorant of Heaven. White men are in Hell. Aye, leave him ignorant of the civilization that sends us there, and the religious men that say it is good to be in that Hell. . . . Send an English Testament to his Grace of Canterbury, and let it consist of that one sentence, at which he winks his eyes:

'Ye have heard that it *hath* been said: An eye for an eye, and a tooth for a tooth:

But I say that ye resist not evil, but whosoever shall smite thee on thy right cheek, turn to him the other also.'

And if his reply be 'Most unsuitable for the present distressing moment, my dear lady! But I trust that in God's good time . . . etc.'—*then there is only one possible conclusion*, that there are no more Christians at the present moment than there were at the end of the first century.

Sassoon also made a direct attack on the Church and its priests in a poem published in *Counter-Attack and Other Poems* in 1918. Like 'Le Christianisme' the starting-point was again a church, but this time an unharmed church in the vicinity of Edinburgh, a church whose joyful bells appeared to ignore and make little of the suffering and death in France:

> *What means this metal in windy belfries hung*
> *When guns are all our need? Dissolve these bells*
> *Whose tones are tuned for peace: with martial tongue*
> *Let them cry doom and storm the sun with shells.*
>
> *Bells are like fierce-browed prelates who proclaim*
> *That 'if our Lord returned He'd fight for us'.*
> *So let our bells and bishops do the same,*
> *Shoulder to shoulder with the motor-bus.*[30]

As has already been pointed out earlier in this chapter, the identification of the soldier-victims with Christ seemed to necessitate the rejection of God and the older generation, the sacrificers, so it is not surprising that the poetry of the realists frequently made harsh or ironic references to these latter. Sassoon attacked the Bishops not only in the poem quoted above, but also in 'They', where the Bishop's facile sermon is brought hard up against the terrible realities of battle; the cruelty and suffering implicit in maiming and death are dismissed with the words, 'The ways of God are strange', an ineffectual apologia for God's helplessness or indifference in war. More positively, Osbert Sitwell showed all the Bishops going 'mad with joy' when a Parliamentary speaker maintained:

> '*Gentlemen, we will never end this war*
> *Till all the younger men with martial mien*
> *Have entered capitals; never make peace*
> *Till they are cripples, on one leg, or dead!*'[31]

Much more common, however, are adverse comments about God the Father. The general burden of these comments is that He is insensible to the sufferings of the soldiers. As early as 1915, Robert Nichols saw God as unwilling to enable one dying soldier to succour another, so that the second one, in his agony 'cursed God and died'.[32] Arthur Graeme West commented in his diary during May 1916:

> If there is a God at all responsible for governing the earth, I hate and abominate Him—I do not think there is one. We only fall into the habit of calling down curses on a god whom we believe not to exist, because the constant references to his beneficence are so maddening that anger stings us to a retort that is really illogical.

In Robert Graves's twentieth-century re-interpretation of the battle between David and Goliath, God dims His eyes, 'His ears are shut', and He allows David to die.[33] In 'Break of Day' Sassoon used the term 'God's blank heart' and Owen spoke in 'Greater Love' of God seeming 'not to care'. However, the poem which most clearly shows the opposition between Christ and God is Owen's 'Soldier's Dream':

> *I dreamed kind Jesus fouled the big-gun gears;*
> *And caused a permanent stoppage in all bolts;*
> *And buckled with a smile Mausers and Colts;*
> *And rusted every bayonet with His tears.*
>
> *And there were no more bombs, of ours or Theirs,*
> *Not even an old flint-lock, nor even a pikel,*
> *But God was vexed, and gave all power to Michael;*
> *And when I woke he'd seen to our repairs.*

Here Christ is seen clearly aligned with the soldiers and working for the relief of their sufferings whilst God is on the other side, once again enforcing the blood sacrifice, the obligatory laying down of life not His own.

· C H A P T E R · S I X ·

⋙⊙⋘⋙⊙⋘⋙⊙⋘

O the mind, mind has mountains; cliffs of fall
Frightful, sheer, no-man-fathomed. Hold them cheap
May who ne'er hung there. Nor does long our small
Durance deal with that steep or deep.

THE THREE PRECEDING chapters have been concerned with the physical, emotional and spiritual aspects of trench warfare. This chapter will consider the various forms of mental distress which are evident in written accounts of the period and which were reflected in the poetry. Broadly speaking, these may be divided into two kinds; first, the mental stresses which, though agonising, can be registered as 'normal' and secondly, the forms of mental illness known variously as shell-shock, war neurosis or neurasthenia, and the psychoses, unrelated to, but probably precipated by, war stress, which in some instances developed into permanent mental imbalance or madness.

The two emotions most significant in producing mental distress were fear and the morbid depression which nurtured guilt. Fear was universal as was readily acknowledged by responsible medical opinion of the time. 'Fear,' it was stated in a report on an official enquiry into shell-shock, 'is an emotion common to all and evidence was given of very brave men who frankly acknowledged it.'[1]

Many years later Lord Moran, writing his book *The Anatomy of Courage*, looked back to the First World War for his examples, and early in the book he commented:

Is there then anyone who does not feel fear? Those who lived in the trenches for a long time may answer by recalling some happy soul who did not appear to be conscious of danger, and had never had to make an effort to carry on. . . . Perhaps he was killed or wounded and was remembered as a man without fear. But if the enemy was less merciful and he was left on his feet, the frailty of the rest of the men overtook

113

him; time had stolen from him his peace of mind that came from a certain vacancy which had always passed for courage.[2]

Certainly in their diaries and letters many men did not hesitate to acknowledge the reality of fear. Arthur Graeme West described in his diary for the 20th of September 1916 how his battalion endured a heavy bombardment in the front-line trenches. It is a frank and moving account:

Men cowered and trembled. . . . Five or six little funk-holes dug into the side of the trench served to take the body of a man in a very huddled and uncomfortable position, with no room to move, simply to cower into the little hole. . . . One simply looks at his hands clasped on his knees, dully and lifelessly, shivering a little as a shell draws near; another taps the side of his hole with his finger-nails, rhythmically; another hides himself in his great-coat and passes into a kind of torpor.

This very explicit and detailed comment, describing not only fear itself, but how men reacted to fear is quite common in diaries where men were writing entirely for themselves. As with many such observations the actual writing down had some sort of therapeutic value at the time. For us today it provides an interesting insight into the way men were thinking and reacting. Less detailed, but equally explicit comments occurred in many letters. Ford Madox Ford, writing to C. F. G. Masterman in January 1917 said that he found himself waking suddenly in the night and lying unable to sleep 'in a hell of a funk till morning'. He added that a good many men were in the same condition. Captain Theodore Wilson in a letter to his mother on the 1st of March 1916 described first the terrible conditions in the trenches where he was and then went on to write of his own feelings under fire:

I was *horribly* afraid—*sick* with fear—not of being hit, but of seeing other people torn, in the way that high explosive tears. It is simply hellish.[3]

Acknowledged fear was, however, the mind's own catharsis. The man who was afraid and knew that he was justified in being afraid and thus was ready to express his fear was less likely to suffer from nervous disorders than the man who repressed his fears:

I think there is an idea among young soldiers especially that there should not be such a thing as fear. I do not know, but I think I was in an awful funk the whole time, and I think most people were, and if the young soldier were given to understand that everybody is very much afraid and that it is a natural condition to be in, but he should overcome it . . . and that it was up to him to control himself, it would have some small effect. Many men are afraid of being thought afraid, and it worries them. I think if it were pointed out that it is not cowardly to be afraid, but it is cowardly to let fear get control of your actions . . . it would help to a certain extent.[4]

In other words, fear itself was not a major problem unless it was continuous and sustained. It is, in fact, clear that men under continuous stress were more susceptible to disturbing emotions than men under intense strain for a brief period. Chapter III discussed the physical discomfort and misery of fatigue. There is no doubt that it also played a supremely important rôle in encouraging the development of neuroses. Lack of sleep and physical exhaustion made men more liable to fear and anxiety; the mental conflict involved in dealing with these fears and anxieties increased the feeling of fatigue. This vicious spiral all too often ended in neurosis.

The real problems were concerned not with men's natural fears, but with the effects which accompanied fear; a man's efforts to pretend that he was not afraid; repression of the causes of fear; the battering of the sensibilities of men whose whole mental outlook was coloured by their attempts not to give way to fear. There was for such men a conflict between fear and their sense of duty; at first such conflict would be consciously appreciated and wrestled with, but when it became intolerable, repression would ensue and neurotic or hysterical symptoms would become manifest.

The psychiatric literature appertaining to the period makes it fairly clear that in most cases of war neurosis the soldier concerned had something in his mental and nervous make-up which made him more liable than others to nervous disorders. However, Dr. Millais Culpin stated quite categorically that:

The percentage of findings of predisposition to mental disturbances . . . signifies that the number of patients whose symptoms are due entirely to war experiences acting upon a mentally sound organism is likely to be small. Nevertheless, the study of a few cases apparently of this type leads me to believe that, given enough of the strain of modern warfare, any man whatsoever will break down.[5]

At the War Office Enquiry into 'Shell-Shock' Dr. W. H. R. Rivers also emphasized the fact that there was

> the man who breaks down after long and continued strain. These were the men who . . . after some shell explosion or something else had knocked them out badly, went on struggling to do their duty until they finally collapsed entirely.[6]

A little later, during the same enquiry, Dr. Rivers accepted the suggestion that men in this condition were probably suffering from a 'mental wound' or 'trauma'.

Today there is very much more lay recognition of mental and nervous disorders, even if they are not properly understood, than there was fifty to sixty years ago. This, however, makes it more difficult for us to accept the line which was then drawn between fear and cowardice, and even more finely, between conscious and un-conscious cowardice, between malingering and hysteria—that is between the man who was afraid and gave way to fear and the man who was afraid and suffered from an anxiety neurosis. It is interesting to find that in the *War Office Enquiry* military witnesses were, on the whole, more willing to differentiate whilst medical witnesses were, in general, less willing:

> Dr. Mapother said: 'Frankly I am not prepared to make a decision between cowardice and shell-shock. Cowardice I take to mean action under the influence of fear and the ordinary type of "shell-shock" was, to my mind, persistent and chronic fear.'

The summing-up of the evidence in this section makes interesting reading:

> *Dr. Hampton:* 'Many cases were on the border line between conscious and unconscious malingering.'

> *Lieut-Colonel Scott Jackson:* 'Many cases of neurasthenia and "shell-shock" were skrimshanking of the worst type.'

> *Major Adie:* 'We did not see much malingering.'

> *Dr. Wilson*, in speaking of men who took advantage of an attack to get away, said: 'I do not know how much malingering there is in these cases; it is almost impossible to tell.'

116

Colonel Campbell considered 'shell-shock' a favourite method which malingerers employed to get away from the battle front . . .

Dr. Dunn said: 'In acute shock a man abandons himself to his terror. I have not seen an attempt to simulate it, and I cannot imagine such an attempt deceiving anyone.'

Colonel Jervis considered the number of emotional breakdowns was slight as compared to the number 'swinging the lead.'[7]

Any distinction would appear to be entirely arbitrary; once hysteria had developed a man was no longer capable of controlling his own actions; on the other hand apparent simulation of hysteria would suggest in itself some lack of conscious control which probably arose from excessive fear. To call actions performed by a man suffering from hysteria or from hysterical simulation, cowardice, and to punish them accordingly showed a complete lack of understanding of the psychiatric problems involved.

It is necessary to dwell upon the questions of fear, cowardice and neurosis, because the problems they raised were not easily soluble; they also provide another instance in which the private soldier and the junior officer were aligned together against the senior officers, staff and those at home. Rank cowardice and 'skrimshanking' were fairly universally condemned but the more experience of trench warfare a man had the more likely he was to feel sympathy with others who had broken under the strain. 'A man has sought refuge in our house, his nerves all gone. He sobbed and moaned a little as each [shell] came' wrote D. H. Bell in his Diary for the 20th of April 1915. Here there is no sign of condemnation for a man who has given way to fear. Similarly, Ralph Scott in his Diary for the 18th of August 1918 asserted angrily,

If ever again I hear any one say anything against a man for incapacitating himself in any way to get out of this I will kill that man. Not even Almighty God can understand the effort required to force oneself back into the trenches at night.

Through his very bluntness and rough soldierly attitude, Frank Richards succeeded admirably in conveying the pity of war in his description of the following incident during the battle of the Somme:

One of our old stretcher-bearers went mad and started to undress himself. He was uttering horrible screams, and we had to fight with him and overpower him before he could be got to the Aid Post. He had been going queer for the last month or two.[8]

On the other hand, Lieutenant-Colonel R. G. A. Hamilton, The Master of Belhaven, was unable to extend any real sympathy or understanding to men suffering from nervous or mental disorders. On the 30th of July 1917 he reported in his diary, 'Another man has gone mad. This makes two since we have been in this position.' Four days later, on the 3rd of August 1917 he made the following report:

Another man has gone off his head, but I have refused to allow him to leave the guns. It is simply a matter of everyone having to control their nerves. I am very sorry for the man, but if the idea once gets about that a man can get out of this hell by letting go of his nerves, Heaven help us.

Within the hierarchical context of war organization the varying attitudes are understandable. The junior officers and private soldiers were concerned with their small area of operations and with the men within that area, most of whom they knew personally and were in close contact with. They were not only aware of the fear and horror of battle and of the immense strain of being under constant bombardment, but they were also directly involved in each other's nervous troubles:

My nerves are under control, and I can do my job all right, but I am feeling the strain in a way I used not to do. I often find myself speaking sharply when there is no need for it. The men too seem different; they no longer want 'Jerry' to come over, as they used to declare.[9]

On the other hand senior officers such as Lieutenant-Colonel Hamilton overlooked a much larger situation. A man who went 'mad' was simply another gap in the firing line; if others became infected by his madness the gaps would become formidable. The private soldier or the junior officer would see a friend or companion breaking; the senior officer merely saw them, as Wilfred Owen described, as

Men, gaps for filling:
Losses, who might have fought
Longer.[10]

118

As has already been stated, simple fear, recognized and expressed, was not generally a cause for neurosis; however, the repression of simple fear and the existence of more complicated fears and anxieties was a major cause of breakdowns among officers. 'The private soldier has to think only or chiefly of himself,' wrote Dr. W. H. R. Rivers,

he has not to bear with him continually the thought that the lives of forty or fifty men are immediately, and of many more remotely, dependent on his success in controlling any expression of fear or apprehension.[11]

Dr. Henry Head made a similar affirmation in his evidence to the War Office Committee of Enquiry:

The officer . . . is repressing all the time because, first of all, he must not show fear in any circumstances. In some circumstances all the men are afraid, therefore he has to repress all that. Then again, he has . . . to think of his men as a father thinks of his children. Therefore, here again he has an enormous responsibility thrown upon him. It is to a great extent anxiety on behalf of others.[12]

So it was often the man with a sense of responsibility who suffered most since not only did he suffer fear but he also had to suffer the anguished possibility of giving way to fear in front of those for whom he was responsible. Lord Moran, describing a sergeant who shot himself at Armentières, commented,

It was plain enough then that he could not face war and was not certain what he might do and had taken the matter into his own hands before he did something dreadful that might bring disgrace on himself and on his regiment.[13]

The thin line which separated the man labelled 'neurasthenic' from the man labelled 'coward' would perhaps not have been important were it not for the fact that cowardice was a military crime punishable by death. The man who gave way to fear risked exchanging the chance of injury or death in battle with the certainty of calculated and cold-blooded death at the hands of his own comrades. Who could truly map out the limits of endurance of another soul if we are to believe the medical evidence quoted above that every man, given enough continuous strain, fear and anxiety, was liable to break?

Herbert Read did not wish to be a realist poet: 'I'd rather write one "pastoral" than a book of this realism,' he wrote in his diary for the 14th of March 1918, 'My heart is not in it: it is too objective.'[14] Yet by 1917 he had begun to wonder whether it was not 'a sacred duty after all "to qaint the horrors".'[15] The result was *Naked Warriors* first published in 1919. Throughout this short book fear plays a predominant part in the minds of Read's protagonists. Read himself was acutely aware of what has been described above as the thin line which appeared to separate the neurasthenic from the coward. 'Fear,' he wrote,

> *Fear is a wave*
> *beating through the air*
> *and on taut nerves impinging*
> *till there it wins*
> *vibrating chords.*
>
> *All goes well*
> *so long as you tune the instrument*
> *to simulate composure.*
>
> *(So you will become*
> *a gallant gentleman.)*
>
> *But when the strings are broken*
> *then you will grovel on the earth*
> *and your rabbit eyes*
> *will fill with the fragments of your*
> *shatter'd soul.*[16]

The simulated composure helps to underline the irony of gallantry: the 'gallant gentleman' is he who can pretend well enough to go on pretending; such, Read implies, is the difference between the brave man and the coward. The brave man is able 'to simulate composure' until death overtakes him; if he breaks under the strain he becomes a coward. The long poem from which 'Fear' is taken culminates in 'The Execution of Cornelius Vane', a moral tale in which Cornelius is punished for his cowardice by death. But at the end where the moral should come is the agonising plea:

> *'What wrong have I done that I should leave these:*
> *The bright sun rising*
> *And the birds that sing?'*

120

Our sympathy is required not for legality and courage but for the erring and fearful victim of war's terrors.

There is rarely reference in the poetry to simple fear, the experiencing of an emotion which ends with the experience itself, for fear was rarely simple. The poets were, in general concerned with the ultimate effects of fear—fear that drove a man to wound himself, to kill himself; or perhaps to be shot for cowardice; fear that snapped the nerves and drove a man to seeming madness. Like Read, both Owen and Sassoon were concerned with the fear which made a man feel that he had come to the end of the road.

In 'S.I.W.'[17] Owen traces the military career of a young soldier from the moment when he leaves home with the encouragement of his family to be brave and to do nothing to disgrace himself. Owen emphasizes the continual strain of week after week, month after month in the midst of battle until

> Courage leaked, as sand
> From the best sand-bags after years of rain.
> But never leave, wound, fever, trench-foot, shock,
> Untrapped the wretch. And death seemed still withheld . . .

So the young soldier found it necessary to accomplish his own death. It is a poem of justification. Fear must have an end or man must make the end of it for himself. He cannot live perpetually in a state of fear. Of this the poem leaves us in no doubt, just as the soldier himself was in no doubt:

> It was the reasoned crisis of his soul
> Against more days of inescapable thrall,
> Against infrangibly wired and blind trench wall
> Curtained with fire, roofed in with creeping fire,
> Slow grazing fire, that would not burn him whole
> But kept him for death's promises and scoff,
> And life's half-promising, and both their riling.

Sassoon too allows no condemning of the 'simple soldier boy' who is driven to kill himself. Condemnation is reserved for the people back at home:

> You smug-faced crowds with kindling eye
> Who cheer when soldier lads march by,
> Sneak home and pray you'll never know
> The hell where youth and laughter go.[18]

121

Each of these poems is concerned with a soldier who, having no apparent inherent weakness, nevertheless found that he had reached the limits of his endurance and could no longer withstand fear. Both poets showed too the man who had reached the same state within himself, yet did not choose the escape route of suicide. Sassoon's 'hero',

> cold-footed, useless swine,
> Had panicked down the trench that night the mine
> Went up at Wicked Corner.[19]

Was he more blameworthy than the soldier who killed himself? than the soldier who was sent down from the front line suffering from neurasthenia? than the soldier who was killed in battle the night before 'the mine/Went up at Wicked Corner'? The questions are open-ended. The sting of the poem lies not in the fact that here was a coward whose mother was made to believe that he died a hero, but that here was a man who died unwillingly, 'blown to small bits', forced in the teeth of his fear to stay in the trenches:

> And no one seemed to care
> Except that lonely woman with white hair.

Hero or anti-hero the result was the same. The poem not only deflates ideas of heroic glory but also emphasizes the indifference of the world to the victims of war.

In 'The Dead-Beat' Owen shows us a soldier, apparently un-wounded, who simply broke down, 'his pluck . . . all gone'. Was he a malingerer? The stretcher-bearers thought so; the doctor thought so. But does one die of malingering as this man died? Edmund Blunden recounted a similar incident in which two soldiers put their heads out of a pillbox and narrowly escaped death from a shell; yet one was scratched by a splinter:

> And out burst terrors that he'd striven to tame,
> A good man, Hoad, for weeks. I'm blown to bits.
> He groans, he screams.
>
> *   *   *
>
> The poor man lay at length and brief and mad
> Flung out his cry of doom; soon ebbed and dumb
> He yielded.[20]

It would seem from the evidence in the poems that both these deaths could be put down to commotional shell-shock, that is, the direct result of concussion caused by the *blast* of shell explosion. The *War Office Enquiry into 'Shell-Shock'* summarized the evidence on commotional shock by stating,

> Most of the witnesses who had front line experience had actually seen men lying dead without visible injury, as a result of the explosion of shells or mines.[21]

Certainly the soldier in Owen's poem was considered a 'stout lad . . . before that strafe' and Sergeant Hoad's apparent madness followed a moment of close proximity to an exploding shell (the splinter-scratch could have been incidental). Yet it is clear that in both cases in the brief period before death there were distinct signs of emotional instability which would normally be seen in emotional shell-shock. The men had reached the limits of their endurance; to those around them it appeared that the strain of continuous fear and terror had killed them.

Fear and the depression which led to guilt have already been mentioned as being the principal emotions leading to war neuroses. Feelings of guilt for the direct actions demanded by war service, however, are not very common. Men who had been brought up to believe that to kill another was both a legal crime and a spiritual sin were now placed in situations where not only did their duty towards the state require them to kill, but also the preservation of their own and their comrades lives often depended on it. It is surprising how rarely revulson against direct face-to-face killing is commented on in letters and diaries. It is the exception rather than the rule to find such statements as the following:

> Personally I still shudder at the idea of sticking six inches of cold steel into another man's body or having his steel stuck into my body, but I shudder merely with the natural instinct of repulsion which is common to at least all educated people.[22]

We must assume that, in general, any outward expression of repulsion was repressed. Dr. Millais Culpin reported one such repression describing it as a 'war dream . . . of a common type':

> Patient dreamed of cutting off a man's head; he said he had a vicious feeling whilst doing it. Association on the feeling recalled his going over the top; bayoneting two Germans and shooting one.[23]

Much more widespread were generalized feelings of guilt: mankind's guilt for all the horrors of war; the guilt of the soldier engaged in war who became convinced that war was wrong, and conversely, (and perversely, for the same man often felt it), the guilt of the man on leave or wounded who wanted to be back in France supporting his comrades.

Once more it seems that the Battle of the Somme was the decisive factor in changing enthusiasm into guilt and bitterness. It was the first major battle fought by a conscripted British army. The majority of cases of neurasthenia and shell-shock dated from mid-1916 onwards. There seemed no likely end to war.

Writing in his diary on the 9th of May 1918 Herbert Read expressed the guilt which many men felt at the continuance of war:

> Most of the prisoners we took were boys under twenty. Our own recent reinforcements were all boys. Apart from uniforms, German and English are alike as two peas: beautiful fresh children. And they are massacred in inconceivable torment.[24]

In *Death of a Hero*, in an interpolation by the narrator frightening in its intensity, Richard Aldington associated mankind in his vision of war-guilt:

> What am I? O God, nothing, less than nothing, a husk, a leaving, a half-chewed morsel on the plate, a reject. But an impersonal vendetta, an unappeased conscience crying in the wilderness, a river of tears in the desert. What right have I to live? Is it five million, is it ten million, is it twenty million? What does the exact count matter? There they are, and we are responsible. Tortures of hell, we are responsible! When I meet an unmaimed man of my generation I want to shout at him: 'How did you escape? How did you dodge it? What dirty trick did you play? Why are you not dead, trickster. . . . You, the war dead, I think you died in vain, I think you died for nothing, for a blast of wind, a blather, a humbug, a newspaper stunt, a politician's ramp. But at least you died. You did not reject the sharp, sweet shock of bullets, the sudden smash of the shell-burst, the insinuating agony of poison gas. You got rid of it all. You chose the better part.'[25]

During the ten years after the war, whilst *Death of a Hero* was gestating, it is clear that Aldington carried around with him his burden of guilt.

Another source of guilt was to be found in the dilemma of the 'pacifist-soldier.' In 1914 many men who had no real belief in the efficacy of war nevertheless became soldiers. During the war, however, their feelings against it were strengthened. At the same time they felt that they could not simply opt out and leave the struggle to others. Hence they were at war, not only with the enemy soldiers, but within their own souls. In addition to the dilemma of conscience there was the fact that a man could be signing his own death warrant if, once in the army, he refused to fight. Arthur Graeme West returned from leave to France in mid-August 1916, convinced that he no longer believed in war:

> I go down in an hour to the pit again, less willingly, more hating it than ever.
> What I have thought and read lately . . . makes me doubt very much if I do well to go. This is the bitterest part of it.
> I do ill to go. I ought to fight no more. But death, I suppose, is the penalty, and public opinion and possible misunderstanding.[26]

One assumes that a gesture from West would have been misunderstood, just as Sassoon's gesture almost a year later was misunderstood and rejected:

> I am making this statement as an act of wilful defiance of military authority, because I believe that the War is being deliberately prolonged by those who have the power to end it. . . . I believe that this War, upon which I entered as a war of defence and liberation, has now become a war of aggression and conquest. . . . I have seen and endured the sufferings of the troops, and I can no longer be a party to prolong these sufferings for ends which I believe to be evil and unjust.[27]

Sassoon's attempts to express his guilt publicly and to withdraw from the war at whatever private cost and ignominy were defeated. He came before a Medical Board and was sent to Craiglockhart Hospital for 'shell-shocked' officers. The irony of this is that he was adjudged to be suffering from war-neurosis because he did not repress his thoughts on war, whereas the principal method of treatment within the hospital was designed to bring back into men's memories the thoughts which they had repressed. However, one must at the same time see the diagnosis on Sassoon as humane. He could have been shot!

It is surprising that in the *War Office Report into 'Shell-Shock'* no mention is made of guilt as a factor contributing to neurosis yet guilt was widely felt, certainly amongst the more articulate men and officers, and the depression which fuels it is an emotion as disturbing to the mental and spiritual balance as is fear.

Wilfred Owen, who was also sent to Craiglockhart Hospital as a neurasthenic, was another 'pacifist-soldier' whose creed was firmly formulated during his first term of duty in the trenches:

Passivity at any price! Suffer dishonour and disgrace; but never resort to arms. Be bullied, be outraged, be killed; but do not kill.[28]

A few lines later in the same letter he asks '. . . am I not myself a conscientious objector with a very seared conscience?' Yet his conscience continued to be seared for his dilemma was inescapable. If he had followed his doctrine of 'Passivity at any price' he might well have suffered dishonour and disgrace but his guilt would have been no less; he would have remembered

> . . . the sighs of men, that have no skill
> To speak of their distress, no, nor the will![29]

and would have felt that he was shirking his duty in not going out to France again in order 'to cry [his] outcry, playing [his] part.[30]

Even a brief absence in comfort and safety from his own company made Edmund Blunden feel guilty. He was directed to go for several weeks on a signalling course; his comment was,

It was wonderful to be promised an *exeat* from war for weeks, but I saw once again the distasteful process of separation from the battalion, and felt as usual the injustice of my own temporary escape while others who had seen and suffered more went on in the mud and muck.[31]

One can see here that the writer's mind was divided against itself: there was joy at his own escape but guilt that he had to leave his company, many of whom appeared to him to deserve escape more. The desire to get back to the company of one's fellow-victims appears to have been common. Lord Moran explained it thus:

When you are in the trenches a cushy wound, a blighty business, seems the most desirable thing in the world, but when you are at the base the time comes sooner or later when you get restless and in the end you are glad to return. The good fellow knows there is something wrong with men who cling to jobs behind, he feels he is becoming one of them, loses his peace of mind and sees at last that in war there is but one thing to do, then he goes and does it . . . Such a man however may and often does loathe every minute of this business.[32]

Feelings of guilt are frequently expressed in the poetry of the period though, as in the other writings, any expression of guilt for performing the necessary actions of war is unusual. Sassoon deals with this aspect of the subject in one terrible poem called 'Remorse':

> . . . he saw those Germans run,
> Screaming for mercy among the stumps of trees:
> Green-faced, they dodged and darted: there was one
> Livid with terror, clutching at his knees . . .
> Our chaps were sticking 'em like pigs . . . 'O hell!'
> He thought—'there's things in war one dare not tell
> Poor father sitting safe at home, who reads
> Of dying heroes and their deathless deeds.'

However, although the poem is called 'Remorse' its emphasis is more on the contrast between the two lives—life in the trenches and life at home—and upon the gulf between them.

Ivor Gurney, in 'The Target', also writes of remorse for killing another but with less bitterness and with less immediacy than there is in Sassoon's poem. However, one can see in this poem Gurney's deep-rooted spiritual bewilderment: his mother worries for him; perhaps the German boy he killed was 'the only son', yet there is no guidance to help the poet through his guilt:

> God keeps still, and does not say
> A word of guidance any way.[33]

Death alone can solve his problems, can set his mother's fears at rest and can allow him to make peace with the German boy he had killed, yet for Gurney death in battle did not come; what came to him was madness—the ultimate result of the continuous strain of guilt and fear upon a man who, without doubt, had an individual susceptibility to mental and nervous disturbance.

Gurney, a number of whose poems have been considered in some detail above (pp. 54–7), joined up early in the war and was sent to France in 1916 in time to be involved in the Battle of the Somme. In April

1917 he was wounded, but instead of being sent home he was sent to a Base Hospital and in less than three months he returned to the Front Line and the terrible Battle of Passchendaele. In August he was severely gassed and at last sent back to Britain, broken in health and spirit, suffering not only acutely from gas poisoning, but also from neurasthenia. The following year he was sent to a mental hospital and discharged from the army. From that time until his death in 1937 he never fully recovered his sanity, though he was lucid for a great deal of the time. The war never left him and his later poetry, though often marred and disordered, bears witness against those responsible for war, the 'They' of 'What's in Time':

> They gave me to Hell black torture as surely
> As God—if He judge them—shall judge for it.
> They tortured my last nerve, and tortured my wit.[34]

There is often a frightening intensity in the disjointed lines which recall Gurney's war experiences, lines written out of the horror of his mental breakdown, trying to apportion blame and responsibility for man's suffering in war; but the reader is forced to grope towards meaning through the words which are themselves a sign of Gurney's affliction, as in the lines 'To Crickley':

> Soldier that knew war's pains, poet
> That kept our love—
> The gods have not saved you, it is not
> Our prayers lacking to move.
>
> Then to you—deep in Hells now still-burning
> For sleep or the end's peace—
> By tears we have not saved you; yearning
> To accusation and our hopes loss turning.[35]

Gurney was, without doubt, the most seriously mentally afflicted of those whose poetry has been considered, but it should perhaps be remembered that a good deal of both Owen's and Sassoon's poetry was written in Craiglockhart War Hospital for Neurasthenic Officers, and that most of the realist poets, even if they survived the war, came out either physically wounded or mentally and emotionally scarred. Richard Aldington, who was gassed towards the end of the war, never regained a completely balanced view of life. The sense of responsibility for the war which led to his heartcry in *Death of a Hero*, quoted above, was reproduced in his poetry. Never again could he know 'pure happiness':[36]

> I was happy.
> It was enough not to be dead,
> Not to be a black spongy mass of decay
> Half-buried on the edge of a trench

but a whisper disturbed his happiness,

> 'This happiness is not yours;
> It is stolen from other men.
> Coward! You have shirked your fate.'[37]

Sassoon too reproduced in poetry his sense of guilt at the continuance of the war. His responsibility as an officer weighed heavily upon him:

> Can they guess
> The secret burden that is always mine?—
> Pride in their courage; pity for their distress;
> And burning bitterness
> That I must take them to the accursed line.[38]

As with Aldington, his pity and responsibility developed into a sense of generalized guilt for the waste, futility and loss of war:

> O martyred youth and manhood overthrown,
> The burden of your wrongs is on my head.[39]

Guilt was probably always stronger away from the trenches than in them. When Aldington finally escaped from the war through being gassed it was at home, playing at love and grasping for happiness, that guilt overcame him. Sassoon, in England on sick leave, dreamed of his comrades who had been killed and felt guilt that he had escaped through a lesser sacrifice:

> 'Why are you here with all your watches ended?
> From Ypres to Frise we sought you in the Line.'
> In bitter safety I awake, unfriended;
> And while the dawn begins with slashing rain
> I think of the Battalion in the mud,
> 'When are you going out to them again?
> Are they not still your brothers through our blood?'[40]

It is interesting to observe that the guilt which Owen expressed was generally of a different kind. It was more a grievance than a personal guilt—a guilt which he wished on to the people at home who 'by choice [had] made themselves immune/To pity.'[41] Unlike Aldington and Sassoon he was less ready to associate himself with this guilt. He did so, however, in two very powerful poems, 'Strange Meeting' and 'Mental Cases'. In the first of these a meeting in Hell with his German *doppelgänger* apparently brought to the poet an awareness of guilt and remorse that two men with the same hopes and aspirations, the same gifts, the same powers should destroy each other and the world's future because they happened to be born in different countries; there was indeed cause to mourn 'the undone years,/The hopelessness'. It is significant that the pity and terror of war, the humanity and the courage are expressed by the dead German, for by this means Owen ensures a ready sympathy with him; it was the German who was reluctant to kill his fellow-man and who thus had himself to die. At the same time, of course, Owen is being confronted with his *alter ego*; inside the poet is the man who stabbed and the man who was stabbed, and he has to come to terms with the sensibilities of both men. It is a poem of universal brotherhood and cannot be read without involving the reader in a sense of guilt at man's 'inhumanity to man'.[42]

Before discussing 'Mental Cases' let us return to a consideration of shell-shock. The most distressing effect of the strain of guilt and fear was the temporary madness or insanity which was the hallmark of the war neurosis. Most men fighting in the trenches had seen the moment when a man went 'all to pieces':

> *His wild heart beats with painful sobs*
> *his strain'd hands clutch an ice-cold rifle*
> *his aching jaws grip a hot parch'd tongue*
> *his wide eyes search unconsciously.*
>
> *He cannot shriek.*
>
> *Bloody saliva*
> *dribbles down his shapeless jacket.*
>
> *I saw him stab*
> *and stab again*
> *a well-killed Boche.*[43]

Most of the realist poets wrote about this kind of inconsequential lunacy, which was to them the outward sign of war neurosis. Again, there is no doubt that most soldiers had seen men suffering from the kind of mental imbalance that Sassoon described in 'Survivors'. Written at Craiglockhart the poem is a very accurate and evocative description of some of his fellow-sufferers, showing both those suffering from hysterical symptoms—hysterical dumbness, hysterical lameness—and those suffering from anxiety neuroses, who experienced fearful dreams and were often haunted by guilt:

> *No doubt they'll soon get well; the shock and strain*
>   *Have caused their stammering, disconnected talk.*
> *Of course they're 'longing to go out again,'—*
>   *These boys with old, scared faces, learning to walk.*
> *They'll soon forget their haunted nights; their cowed*
>   *Subjection to the ghosts of friends who died,—*
> *Their dreams that drip with murder.*

Yet there is a certain ambivalence in Sassoon's attitude here: 'No doubt they'll soon get well . . . They'll soon forget . . .' The irony is obvious; they were the words of the sacrificers, not of the victims; but they must also have been the words of Dr. Rivers whom Sassoon admired and trusted, for the general summary of medical evidence in the *War Office Enquiry into 'Shell-Shock'* asserted that

From the evidence before the Committee, they are of opinion that there is no justification for the popular belief that 'shell-shock' was a direct cause of insanity, or that the service patients still in asylums were originally cases of 'shell-shock' who have since become insane.[44]

None of the medical evidence in this Report suggested that permanent insanity could develop from 'shell-shock', though it was acknowledged that many 'shell-shock' cases suffered from temporary confusional insanity, which normally disappeared within a day or so, and in almost every case within two weeks. The chronic cases were, in fact, seen to be suffering (perhaps simultaneously with some form of neurasthenia) from mental disorders which did not have their origins in war conditions, though symptoms may well have appeared through the stresses of war. We must assume that this evidence is probably true, but we must also realize that it was not evidence that was public knowledge. It seemed to the soldiers fighting in the war that many of their comrades had been driven mad by the strains and stresses of their military lives. That they would, in fact, recover, or, alternatively that their madness had its origins in causes other than war was in a way immaterial. The presence of madness was a fact:

> *I'm going crazy;*
> *I'm going stark, staring mad because of the guns.*[45]
>
> *Children, with eyes that hate you, broken and mad.*[46]
>
> *. . . poor young Jim, 'e's' livin' an' 'e's not;*
> *'E's wounded, killed, and pris'ner, all the lot,*
> *The bloody lot all rolled in one. Jim's mad.*[47]

In a letter to his mother on the 25th of May 1918 Wilfred Owen mentioned his 'terrific poem . . . "The Deranged"'. This poem became 'Mental Cases'. It is a clear statement of connection between guilt and insanity and, progressing further, between insanity and guilt. Though medical evidence might refute it, to sensitive men like Owen the connection seemed to be clear: guilt for the crimes of war could, and demonstrably did, drive men mad:

> *Who are these? Why sit they here in twilight?*
> *Wherefore rock they, purgatorial shadows,*
> *Drooping tongues from jaws that slob their relish,*
> *Baring teeth that leer like skulls' teeth wicked?*
> *Stroke on stroke of pain,—but what slow panic,*
> *Gouged these chasms round their fretted sockets?*
> *Ever from their hair and through their hands' palms*
> *Misery swelters.*

The description is realistic, horrible, and suggests far more convincingly than Sassoon's poem, 'Survivors', quoted above, that these mental cases will not recover sanity. And the cause of their madness is their guilt for all the cruelties and futilities of war:

> *—These are men whose minds the Dead have ravished*
> *Memory fingers in their hair of murders,*
> *Multitudinous murders they once witnessed.*
> *Wading sloughs of flesh these helpless wander,*
> *Treading blood from lungs that had loved laughter.*

The chain of reaction does not end there, however, for guilt is returned upon those who, by their very existence in time of war, allowed war to occur:

> *. . . their hands are plucking at each other;*
> *Picking at the rope-knots of their scourging;*
> *Snatching after us who smote them, brother,*
> *Pawing us who dealt them war and madness.*

The last two lines of the poem revert to the theme of universal brotherhood, but it is a brotherhood in guilt, involving all those who are not the 'mental cases'. It was Man who 'dealt them war and madness'.

· E P I L O G U E ·

From those appalled and personal throes
Time will dissolve the pain, one knows;
And days when direful news was heard
Be indistinct, unreal, and blurred.

THE 11th OF NOVEMBER 1918. In France a Signals message told the troops that the war had come to an end:

> Hostilities will cease at 1100 on Nov 11th. Troops will stand fast on line reached at that hour which will be reported to this Office. Defensive precautions will be maintained. There will be no intercourse of any description with the enemy.

At home the church bells rang, flags were waved and people flocked into the streets shouting and cheering. But a sour note creeps into almost all the accounts of Armistice Day by those who had actually fought in the war. Joy there certainly was; it was expressed in straightforward terms by Will Judy in his diary for the 11th of November 1918:

> The war is ended; everybody is shouting in happiness. Hardships and dangers have gone. We can now come out of our holes in the ground and breathe the air like free men. Let them sign any terms of peace they wish; we want to be natural, life-loving human beings again.

The next day he was still full of the thoughts of peace:

> The world seems changed. When we look into the sky or walk to the top of the hill, or stand on an open road, we have no fear; today we stand up, stretch our arms, look everywhere, and speak with happy voice.

Perhaps the fact that Judy was an American made his joy more exuberant than that of most Englishmen. America had experienced only nineteen months of war.

> *The long, forlorn, relentless trend*
> *From larger day to huger night*[1]

had for the Americans been less long and correspondingly less forlorn and relentless.

For most Englishmen rejoicing was hardly a part of the emotions they experienced on Armistice Day. 'It is over', wrote Ralph Scott simply,

> These last few days I have hardly dared to hope for it, and now that it has come I can hardly realize exactly what it means.

Frank Richards's main feelings were of gratitude that the war had come to an end and that he was not maimed, but his awareness of those who had suffered appears to preclude joy:

> [I was] thankful that I was not blind, that I had my limbs, that I was not horribly disfigured and that I was not an inmate in a mental home like tens of thousands of poor men.[2]

D. H. Bell also felt gratitude, but mingled with it were fears for the future and sadness about the past:

> Thank God the end of the awful blind waste and brutality of war has come, and let us pray it may never return. Man prays to God, because he feels instinctively there is a power outside himself, yet the answer to such prayer depends on man himself. After this lesson is man too little-minded and forgetful to banish the things that cause war?
>
> I am feeling rather ill and depressed, in spite of all the rejoicing around me; immeasurably relieved, glad to be alive and glad we have won, but tired and a little sad.

In *Siegfried's Journey* Sassoon describes the shouting and flag-waving in London on Armistice Day and tells how he hated it and wanted to be alone, yet how some compulsion led him to go to an Armistice party with a friend and how he almost quarrelled with the loud-mouthed civilians there.[3] Herbert Read too felt the need to get away from everyone:

> When the Armistice came . . . I had no feelings, except possibly of self-congratulation. . . . There were misty fields around us, and perhaps a

pealing bell to celebrate our victory. But my heart was numb and my mind dismayed: I turned to the fields and walked away from all human contacts.[4]

So much then, for the immediate reactions to the Armistice. But the First World War seemed to change the men who fought in it as the Second World War did not. In the period between the wars those who had fought, particularly in France, seemed not to recover normality:

> . . . they had not come back the same men. Something had altered in them. They were subject to queer moods, queer tempers, fits of profound depression alternating with a restless desire for pleasure. . . . Something seemed to have snapped in them, their will-power.[5]

Writer after writer expressed the feeling of lassitude and enervation which had overcome them. They had put all their energies, all their efforts into war and now there was nothing left:

> I am weary and tired of life myself; a mere shell of a man, without health or strength, whose vitality was eaten out by the Flanders mud

wrote Ralph Scott, almost two years after the war had ended.[6] Edmund Blunden saw his post-war self as no longer a sentient being. All emotions, all relationships were exhausted in France and though he was physically alive his real self was 'Dead as the men [he] loved'; only the past had life:

> Tired with dull grief, grown old before my day,
> I sit in solitude and only hear
> Long silent laughters, murmurings of dismay,
> The lost intensities of hope and fear.[7]

Sassoon too gave the impression of being played out physically and spiritually. His vision is of a self left behind in France:

> I seem to write these words of someone who never returned from France, someone whose effort to succeed in that final experience was finished when he lay down in the sunken road and wondered what he ought to say.[8]

Scott Fitzgerald, whose war service, it is true, was rather brief, nevertheless blamed the spirit which pervaded the world after the war for his own lack of vitality:

After all life hasn't much to offer except youth and . . . every man I've met who's been to war, that is this war, seems to have lost youth and faith in man.[9]

It seemed that the experience of war had completely drained the men who returned from it. 'The war bled the world white,' wrote Wyndham Lewis.[10] All their energies and emotions had been used up. The simplicities of life were tinged with past memories and bound up with the experience of war so that wherever their thoughts turned, war intervened:

> *We who are left, how shall we look again*
> *Happily on the sun, or feel the rain,*
> *Without remembering how they who went*
> *Ungrudgingly, and spent*
> *Their all for us, loved, too, the sun and rain?*
>
> *A bird among the rain-wet lilac sings—*
> *But we, how shall we turn to little things*
> *And listen to the birds and winds and streams*
> *Made holy by their dreams,*
> *Nor feel the heart-break in the heart of things?*[11]

Men had been altered by what they had seen and done and nothing in the peace offered them consolation. Many had a presentiment, in some cases a conviction, that peace was a mere interim, that the lessons of 1914–18 would be forgotten. Already in March 1919 Siegfried Sassoon was asking,

> *Have you forgotten yet? . . .*
> For the world's events have rumbled on since
>   those gagged days,
>
>   *   *   *
>
> *But the past is just the same—and War's a bloody game . . .*
> *Have you forgotten yet? . . .*
> *Look down, and swear by the slain of the war that you'll*
>   *never forget.*
>
>   *   *   *
>
> Do you ever stop and ask, 'Is it all going to happen again?'
>
>   *   *   *
>
> *Have you forgotten yet? . . .*
> *Look up, and swear by the green of the spring that you'll*
>   *never forget.*[12]

Osbert Sitwell too appeared to have little faith in the idea of lasting peace for he saw the 'alchemists/Who had converted blood into gold' preparing to create a memorial for those who had died in the war, and

> *'What more fitting memorial for the fallen*
> *Than that their children*
> *Should fall for the same cause?'* ...
> *And the children*
> *Went.*[13]

The cynicism of Sitwell and the prophetic nature of the fears of many of those who had survived the war was demonstrated in 1939, for peace had not yet come of age when the post-war generation were called to follow in their father's footsteps. And—as Sitwell had foreseen—'the children/Went'.

·NOTES·

~·⋗○⋖·⋗○⋖·⋗○⋖·~

These notes should be used in conjunction with the Bibliography which gives full details of all texts used. See Prefatory Note (p. 14) for further clarification.

Introductory

Epigraph. Viscount Gray of Fallodon. See *Twenty-Five Years*, vol. 2, ch. 18.

1. 'How a World War Began'—2. *Observer*, 23 November 1958.
2. 'How a World War Began'—3. *Observer*, 30 November 1958.
3. '1914'.
4. *Mons, Anzac and Kuts*, p. 48.
5. Report from a doctor at a Military Hospital in France. *The Times*, 22 December 1914.
6. *The First World War*, p. 140.
7. *The Contrary Experience*, p. 213.
8. C. R. M. F. Cruttwell. *A History of the Great War*, p. 442.
9. Frank Owen. *Tempestuous Journey*, p. 442.
10. Charles Sorley. 'When you see millions of the mouthless dead'.

Chapter I

Epigraph. Wordsworth. 'Character of the Happy Warrior'.

1. 'For a Trafalgar Cenotaph'.
2. 'Clifton Chapel'.
3. *The Complete Memoirs of George Sherston*, p. 502.
4. 'Sonnets 1914. II. Safety'.
5. *A Student in Arms*, p. 91.

6. Housman. *War Letters of Fallen Englishmen*, p. 158.
7. Housman. *op. cit.*, p. 284f.
8. In this and the following poem * * * indicate substantial omissions.
9. Hardy's 1903 Preface to *The Dynasts*, part 1.
10. See note 8.
11. *The Cornhill* XLI, 244. New Series (October 1916).
12. 'Youth in the War'. *The Cornhill* XLII, 248. New Series (February 1917).
13. Rupert Brooke. 'Sonnets 1914. I. Peace'. ✓
14. *Disenchantment*, p. 210.
15. Introduction to *Anthology of War Poetry*, p. 27.
16. W. N. Hodgson. 'Labuntur Anni'; * * * indicate a substantial omission.
17. *Keeling Letters and Recollections*, p. 179f.
18. p. 69.
19. *A Soldier's Diary of the Great War*, p. 54.
20. Housman. *War Letters*, p. 117f.
21. *Anthology of War Poetry*, p. 21.
22. *op. cit.*, p. 25. Nichols's quotation is from Wordsworth's *The Prelude* (1850), 11. 108–9.
23. *op. cit.*, p. 35.
24. *The First World War*, p. 56.
25. *The Contrary Experience*, p. 90.
26. 'All the hills and vales along'; * * * indicate a substantial omission.
27. See I. M. Parsons (ed.). *Men who March Away; * * * indicate* a substantial omission.
28. Gibbs. *Now It Can Be Told*, p. 395.
29. *Collected Works*, p. 305.
30. *Goodbye To All That*, p. 240.
31. Housman. *War Letters*, p. 68.
32. Housman. *op. cit.*, p. 156f.
33. John Buchan. *Francis and Riversdale Grenfell*, p. 208.
34. Introduction to *An Anthology of War Poems*. Ed. F. Brereton, p. 14f.
35. Brereton. *An Anthology*, p. 97.
36. *The Complete Memoirs of George Sherston*, p. 220.
37. *op. cit.*, p. 257.
38. Housman. War Letters, p. 197.
39. *Ardours and Endurances*, p. 8.
40. Brereton. *An Anthology*, p. 144; * * * indicate a substantial omission.

41. 'To a Friend Killed in Action'.
42. *Ardours and Endurances*, p. 50.
43. *The Complete Poems*.

Chapter II

Epigraph. Milton. *Paradise Lost*, 1

1. From *Collected Poems*, 1950 254–5. All poems by Yeats which are referred to may be found in this volume unless otherwise specified.

2. This and all poems by Eliot which are referred to may be found in *Collected Poems, 1909–1962*.

3 Quoted in Blunden's notes to his edition of Owen's poems, p. 125. This letter does not appear in Owen's *Collected Letters*.

4. *The Letters of Charles Sorley*, p. 292.

5. *Goodbye To All That*, p. 295.

6. 13 March 1915. Bell's quotation is from *The Winter's Tale*, IV.iii.

7. *Undertones of War*, p. 119.

8. Housman. *War Letters*, p. 296.

9. *The Contrary Experience*, p. 95.

10. Brereton. *An Anthology*, p. 151.

11. 'Returning, We Hear the Larks'.

12. Brereton. *An Anthology*, p. 103.

13. Brereton. *op. cit.*, p. 150.

14. 'Back to Rest'.

15. Brereton. *An Anthology*, p. 98.

16. *Fairies and Fusiliers*, p. 68f.

17. It is interesting to notice the similarity in vocabulary between this poem and Sassoon's much-anthologized 'The Death-Bed'. Particularly striking is the likeness between 'something . . . squat and bestial' and 'blots of green and purple in his eyes' of 'Haunted' and 'pain/Leapt like a prowling beast' and 'Queer blots of colour, purple, scarlet, green,/Flickered and faded in his drowning eyes' of 'The Death-Bed'.

18. *Songs of Peace*, 1917 and *Last Songs*, 1918; a third volume, *Songs of the Fields*, although published in 1916, was completed by June 1914.

19. 'For the Fallen (September 1914)'.

20. *Last Songs*, p. 58f.

21. All these quotations are taken from Thomas's *Collected Poems*, 1965.
22. ∗ ∗ ∗ represent a substantial omission.
23. From *War's Embers*.
24. From *Severn and Somme*.
25. This, and the next quotation are from *Poems*, (ed. Blunden).

Chapter III

Epigraph. Wordsworth. *The Borderers*, Book 3.

1. *The Times*, 5 November 1915.
2. *A Soldier's Diary of the Great War*, p. 59f.
3. *op. cit.*, 1 October 1915.
4. 7 October 1915.
5. MS Letter.
6. *Undertones of War*, p. 135.
7. *Surprised by Joy*. Fontana edition, p. 157.
8. *De Bello Germanico*, p. 72.
9. p. 55.
10. Foulkes. '*Gas!*', p. 143.
11. Philip Gibbs. *Now It Can Be Told*, p. 8.
12. R. C. MacFie. *War*, p. 39.
13. 'The Dream'.
14. 'Bombardment'.
15. 'The Immortals'; the second stanza of this poem has been omitted.
16. *The Contrary Experience*, p. 213.
17. 'They'.
18. 'Gethsemane'; ∗ ∗ ∗ represent a substantial omission.
19. 'Dulce et Decorum Est'.
20. *The Diary of a Dead Officer*, p. 67.
21. *The Diary of a Dead Officer*, p. 82.
22. *Undertones of War*, p 289.

Chapter IV

Epigraph. St John XV. 13.

1. Donald Hankey. *Letters*, p. 434.
2. *Francis and Riversdale Grenfell*, p. 223.

3. *Undertones of War*, p. 154.
4. Housman. *War Letters*, p. 107.
5. From *The Wipers Times and After*. 'Wipers' was the name the Tommies gave to Ypres.
6. *Fairies and Fusiliers*, p. 7.
7. *War's Embers*, p. 62; * * * represent a substantial omission.
8. * * * represent a substantial omission.
9 *Ardours and Endurances*, p. 44; * * * represent a substantial omission.
10. 'Owen Agonistes'.
11. p. 218.
12. p. 225.
13. p. 26.
Epigraph to section 2. St Luke X. 29.
14. Housman. *War Letters*, p. 118.
15. p. 65.
16. p. 351.
17. p. 95.
18. *Letters and Recollections*, p. 260.
19. Housman. *War Letters*, p. 290.
20. Housman. *op. cit.*, p. 294.
21. p. 145.
22. *The Soul of the War*, p. 124f.
23. 3 September 1918.
24. 'The Scene of War. V. Liedholz'.
25. *The Diary of a Dead Officer*, p. 79f.
26. Brereton. *An Anthology*, p. 62f.
27. *vide supra*, p. 32.
28. 24 November 1914.
29. *The Complete Memoirs of George Sherston*, p. 387.
30. 'Epitaphs of the War: Batteries out of Ammunition'.
31. *Now It Can Be Told*, p. 534.
32. Housman. *War Letters*, p. 72f.
33. 21 November 1914.
34. *Now It Can Be Told*, p. 143.
35. Preface to *Anthology of War Poetry*, p. 58f.
36. *De Bello Germanico*, p. 81.
37. *Old Soldiers Never Die*, p. 170.
38. *Soldier Poets*, p. 76. Campbell's line, 'Let us think of them that sleep', comes from 'The Battle of the Baltic'.

39. From Brian Gardner (ed.). *Up the Line to Death*, p. 111f. * * * represent a substantial omission.
40. See Brereton. *An Anthology*, p. 90.
41. Quoted in 'Castor and Pollux, Julian and Billy Grenfell' in *The New Elizabethans* by E. B. Osborn, p. 304f.

Chapter V

Epigraph. Edmund Burke. *Reflections on the Revolution in France*.

1. The term 'Christian myth' is used to describe the whole aura of narrative and belief that conventionally attaches itself to the story of the birth, life and death of Christ. It is not in itself a statement of disbelief.
2. Housman. *War Letters*, p. 35.
3. p. 107.
4. Philip Gibbs. *Now It Can Be Told*, p. 142.
5. p. 103f.
6. *Soldier Poets*, p. 67.
7. Brereton. *An Anthology*, p. 149.
8. *Ardours and Endurances*, p. 54.
9. Edmund Blunden. *Undertones of War*, p. 138.
10. *War's Embers*, p. 92.
11. Brereton. *An Anthology*, p. 86.
12. 'Spring Offensive'.
13. *Severn and Somme*, p. 66.
Epigraph to section 2. Genesis XXII. 2.
14. cf. St John III. 16.
15. *Goodbye To All That*, p. 102.
16. Wilfred Owen. 'The Parable of the Old Man and the Young
17. *Argonaut and Juggernaut*, p. 106.
18. *Goodbye To All That*, p. 288.
19. Housman. *War Letters*, p. 171.
20. *Collected Letters*, p. 461.
21. Housman. *War Letters*, p. 176.
22. Quoted in Sitwell. *Noble Essences*, p. 105.
23. *Collected Letters*, p. 562. In transcribing this letter from *Noble Essences* the editors included a superfluous 'to see' beween 'his feet' and 'that'; I have kept to the original text.
24. *Argonaut and Juggernaut*, p. 104.

25. *op. cit.*, p. 110.
26. MS letter to his mother and father 3 December 1915.
27. *Ardours and Endurances*, p. 33f.
28. 'At a Calvary near the Ancre'.
29. 'Le Christianisme'.
30. 'Joy-Bells'.
31. *Argonaut and Juggernaut*, p. 117.
32. *Invocation*, p. 40.
33. *Fairies and Fusiliers*, p. 12.

Chapter VI

Epigraph. Gerard Manley Hopkins. 'No worst, there is none'.
1. *Report of the War Office Committee of Enquiry into 'Shell-Shock'*, p. 139.
2. p. 10.
3. Housman. *War Letters*, p. 295.
4. *War Office Enquiry*, p. 47.
5. *Psychoneuroses of War and Peace*, p. 122.
6. p. 55.
7. p. 144. Of those with military titles, Major Adie was a distinguished physician and neurologist serving as a Medical Officer in the R.A.M.C. The others all held high military positions, though Lieut-Colonel Scott Jackson appears to have had a medical degree. However, he was not serving as a Medical Officer, but in a military capacity.
8. *Old Soldiers Never Die*, p. 186.
9. Bell. *A Soldier's Diary*, p. 152.
10. 'Insensibility'.
11. *Instinct and the Unconscious*, p. 219.
12. p 70.
13. *The Anatomy of Courage*, p. 191.
14. *The Contrary Experience*, p. 122.
15. *op. cit.*, p. 112.
16. 'The Scene of War. III. Fear'.
17. 'S.I.W.' stands for 'Self-Inflicted Wound'; they were the letters written on the medical or death certificate of a soldier so wounded or killed.
18. 'Suicide in the Trenches'.
19. 'The Hero'.

20. *Undertones of War*, p. 293; ∗ ∗ ∗ represent a substantial omission.
21. p. 103.
22. Housman. *War Letters*, p. 58f.
23. *Psychoneuroses of War and Peace*, p. 63.
24. *The Contrary Experience*, p. 128.
25. p. 227.
26. *The Diary of a Dead Officer*, p. 54.
27. *The Complete Memoirs of George Sherston*, p. 496.
28. *Collected Letters*, p 461.
29. Owen. 'The Calls'.
30. *Collected Letters*, p. 568.
31. *Undertones of War*, p. 252.
32. *The Anatomy of Courage*, p. 114.
33. *War's Embers*, p. 50.
34. *Poems*, (ed. Blunden), p. 35.
35. *Poems*, (ed. Clarke), p. 74.
36. From Owen. 'Happiness'.
37. 'In the Palace Garden'.
38. 'The Dream'.
39. 'Autumn'.
40. 'Sick Leave'.
41. 'Insensibility'.
42. Robert Burns. 'Man Was Made To Mourn'.
43. Read. *Collected Poems*, p. 35.
44. p. 145.
45. Sassoon. 'Repression of War Experience'.
46. Sassoon. 'Survivors'.
47. Owen. 'The Chances'.

Epilogue

Epigraph. Sassoon. 'A 1940 Memory'.

1. Owen. 'Insensibility'.
2. *Old Soldiers Never Die*, p. 320f.
3. p. 97f.
4. *The Contrary Experience*, p. 219.
5. Philip Gibbs. *Now It Can Be Told*, p. 547f.
6. *A Soldier's Diary*. 30 August 1920.
7. '1916 Seen from 1921'. From *Poems 1914–30*.
8. *The Complete Memoirs of George Sherston*, p. 650.

9. From A. Mizener. *The Far Side of Paradise*, p. 69.
10. *Blasting and Bombardiering*, p. 18.
11. W. W. Gibson. 'A Lament'.
12. 'Aftermath'; * * * represent substantial omissions.
13. 'The Next War'. *Argonaut and Juggernaut*, p. 122f.

·BIBLIOGRAPHY·

The bibliography is divided into three sections:
A. Manuscripts and Typescripts; B. Primary sources;
C. Secondary sources. Place of publication London, unless otherwise stated.

A. Manuscripts and Typescripts

Anstruther, Fife
Caseby, Alexander. 68 MS pages and corresponding number of pages of photographs, etc. *My Experiences as an Artilleryman with the famous 24th Division.* Owned by the Reverend Alexander Caseby.

Dundee
Longden, A. A. T/s Report. 'Narrative of Operations carried out by 100 Siege Battery Between April 7th and April 14th 1918'. Owned by Mr. James Craigie.

'Wire from 52nd Division'. One of the original Signals' messages which declared the Armistice. Owned by Dr. Hilda D. Spear.

Kirkcaldy, Fife
Burgon, William. 4 MS Letters. December 1915 and January 1916. Owned by Mrs. Elizabeth Burgon Barriss.

Imperial War Museum, London
Byett, Harry. T/s War Diary. December 1914 and January 1915.

British Museum, London
Owen, Wilfred. 2 vols MSS. Vol. 1 contains 53 folios; vol. 2 contains 183 folios. BM Additional MSS 43720 and 43721.

B. Primary Sources

ALDINGTON, Richard. *Images of War*. Beaumont Press. 1919.

—. *Images of War*. (enlarged ed.). Allen and Unwin. 1919.

—. *Death of a Hero*. Chatto and Windus. 1929.

—. *The Complete Poems*. Allen Wingate. 1948. (Text used for poems).

BARBUSSE, Henri. *Le Feu*. Ernest Flammarion. Paris. 1917.

BELL, Douglas Herbert. *A Soldier's Diary of the Great War*. Ed. Henry Williamson. Faber and Gwyer. 1929.

BINYON, Laurence. *Collected Poems*. 2 vols. Macmillan. 1931.

BLUNDEN, Edmund. *Undertones of War*. Cobden-Sanderson. 1928.

—. *De Bello Germanico*. Privately printed. Hawstead. 1930.

—. *Poems, 1914–1930*. Cobden-Sanderson. 1930.

BRERETON, Frederick (ed.). *An Anthology of War Poems*. Collins. 1930.

BROOKE, Rupert. *1914 and Other Poems*. Sidgwick and Jackson. 1915.

—. *Collected Poems*. Sidgwick and Jackson. 1918. (First published by John Lane Company. New York. 1915).

—. *Poetical Works*. Ed. Sir G. Keynes. Faber and Faber. 1946. (Text used for poems).

—. *The Letters of Rupert Brooke*. Ed. Sir G. Keynes. Faber and Faber. 1968.

BUCHAN, John. *Francis and Riversdale Grenfell, A Memoir*. Nelson. 1920.

EDMONDS, Charles (i.e. C. E. Carrington). *A Subaltern's War*. Peter Davies. 1929.

ELIOT, T. S. *Prufrock and Other Observations*. The Egoist Ltd. 1917.

—. *The Waste Land*. Boni and Liveright. New York. 1922.

—. *The Waste Land*. Hogarth Press. 1923.

—. *Collected Poems, 1909–1962*. Faber and Faber. 1963. (Text used).

ELLIS, John. *Eye Deep in Hell*. Croom Helm. 1976.

FORD, Ford Madox (i.e. Ford Madox Hueffer). *On Heaven and Other Poems*. Bodley Head. 1918.

—. *Letters of Ford Madox Ford*. Ed. R. M. Ludwig. Princeton University Press. Princeton, N.J. 1965.

GARDNER, Brian (ed.). *Up the Line to Death*. Eyre Methuen. 1964.

Georgian Poetry, 1911–1912. The Poetry Bookshop. 1912.

—. *1913–1915*. The Poetry Bookshop. 1915.

—. *1916–1917*. The Poetry Bookshop. 1917.

—. *1918–1919*. The Poetry Bookshop. 1919.

GIBBS, Philip (later Sir). *The Soul of the War*. Heinemann. 1915.

GIBBS, Philip (later Sir). *Now It Can Be Told*. Harper. New York. 1920.

—. The above published as *The Realities of War*. Heinemann. 1920.

GIBSON, W. W. *Collected Poems, 1905–1925*. Macmillan. 1926.

GRAVES, Robert. *Over the Brazier*. The Poetry Bookshop. 1916.

—. *Fairies and Fusiliers*. Heinemann. 1917.

—. *Goodbye To All That*. Jonathan Cape. 1929. (Text used).

—. The above: rev. ed. Cassell. 1957; Penguin Books. 1960.

—. *Collected Poems, 1975*. Cassell. 1975.

GURNEY, Ivor. *Severn and Somme*. Sidgwick and Jackson. 1917.

—. *War's Embers*. Sidgwick and Jackson. 1919.

—. *Poems*. Ed. Edmund Blunden. Hutchinson. 1954.

—. *Poems*. Ed. Leonard Clark. Chatto and Windus. 1973.

HAMILTON, R. G. A., Master of Belhaven. *The Diary of the Master of Belhaven, 1914–1918*. John Murray. 1924.

HANKEY, Donald. *A Student in Arms*. Andrew Melrose. 1916.

—. *A Student in Arms*. 2nd series. Andrew Melrose. 1917.

—. *Letters*. Ed. Edward Miller. Andrew Melrose. 1919.

HARDY, Thomas. *The Poetical Works*. 2 vols. Macmillan. 1919.

HAY, Ian, *The First Hundred Thousand*. Blackwood and Sons. Edinburgh. 1915.

HERBERT, Aubrey. *Mons, Anzac and Kuts*. Hutchinson. 1919.

HODGSON, William Noel. *Verse and Prose in Peace and War*. Smith, Elder and Co. 1916.

HOUSMAN, Laurence (ed.). *War Letters of Fallen Englishmen*. Gollancz. 1930.

JONES, David. *In Parenthesis*. Faber and Faber. 1937.

JUDY, Will. *A Soldier's Diary*. Judy Publishing Co. Chicago. 1930.

KEELING, F. H. *Keeling Letters and Recollections*. Ed. E. T. Allen and Unwin. 1918.

KIPLING, Rudyard. *Rudyard Kipling's Verse, 1885–1932*. 1st edition, *1885–1912*. Hodder and Stoughton. 1912. 4th enlarged edition, 1933. (Text used).

LEDWIDGE, Francis. *Songs of Peace*. Herbert Jenkins. 1917.

—. *Last Songs*. Herbert Jenkins. 1918.

LEWIS, Percy Wyndham. *Blasting and Bombardiering*. Eyre and Spottiswoode. 1937.

MACFIE, R. C. *War*. John Murray. 1918.

MANNING, Frederic. *Her Privates We*. Peter Davies. 1930.

—. *The Middle Parts of Fortune* (being the unexpurgated edition of above). Peter Davies. 1977. Mayflower Books. 1977.

MONCRIEFF, C. K. Scott. *Memories and Letters*. Ed. J. M. Scott Moncrieff and L. W. Lunn. Chapman and Hall. 1931.

MONTAGUE, C. E. *Disenchantment*. Chatto and Windus. 1922.

MOYNIHAN, Michael (ed.). *People At War*. David and Charles. Newton Abbot. 1973.

—. *A Place Called Armageddon: Letters from the Great War*. David and Charles. Newton Abbot. 1975.

NEWBOLT, Sir Henry. *Poems New and Old*. John Murray. 1912.

NICHOLS, Robert. *Invocation: War Poems and Others*. Elkin Matthews. 1915.

—. *Ardours and Endurances*. Chatto and Windus. 1917.

—. (ed.). *Anthology of War Poetry, 1914–1918*. Nicholson and Watson. 1943.

OSBORN, E. B. *The New Elizabethans*. John Lane. 1919.

OWEN, Wilfred. *Poems*. Ed. Siegfried Sassoon. Chatto and Windus. 1920.

—. *The Poems of Wilfred Owen*. Ed. Edmund Blunden. Chatto and Windus. 1931.

—. *Collected Poems*. Ed. C. Day Lewis. Chatto and Windus. 1963. (Text used for poems).

—. *War Poems and Others*. Ed. Dominic Hibberd. Chatto and Windus. 1973.

—. *Collected Letters*. Ed. Harold Owen and John Bell. O.U.P. 1967.

PARSONS, Ian (ed.). *Men Who March Away*. Chatto and Windus. 1965.

READ, Herbert (later Sir). *Naked Warriors*. Art and Letters. 1919·

—. *In Retreat*. L. and V. Woolf. 1925.

—. *Annals of Innocence and Experience*. Faber and Faber. 1940.

—. *Collected Poems*. Faber and Faber. 1946. (Text used).

—. *The Contrary Experience*. Secker and Warburg. 1963.

Report of the War Office Committee of Enquiry into 'Shell-Shock'. H.M.S.O. 1922.

RICHARDS, Frank. *Old Soldiers Never Die*. Faber and Faber. 1933.

ROSENBERG, Isaac. *Poems*. Heinemann. 1922.

—. *Collected Works*. Ed. Gordon Bottomley and Denys Harding. Chatto and Windus. 1937.

—. *Collected Poems*. Ed. Gordon Bottomley and Denys Harding. (Revised edition of part of *Collected Works*). Chatto and Windus. 1949. (Text used for poems).

—. *Isaac Rosenberg 1890–1918*. A Catalogue of an Exhibition held at Leeds University. Leeds. 1959.

ROSENBERG, Isaac. *Isaac Rosenberg. A Poet and Painter of the First World War*. A Catalogue of an Exhibition held at the National Book League. London. 1975.

SASSOON, Siegfried. *The Old Huntsman and Other Poems*. Heinemann. 1917.

—. *Counter-Attack and Other Poems*. Heinemann. 1918.

—. *Picture Show*. Privately Printed. Cambridge. 1919.

—. *Memoirs of a Fox-Hunting Man*. Faber and Faber. 1928.

—. *Memoirs of an Infantry Officer*. Faber and Faber. 1930.

—. *Sherston's Progress*. Faber and Faber. 1936.

—. *The Complete Memoirs of George Sherston*. (i.e. the three volumes listed immediately above). Faber and Faber. 1937. (Text used for prose).

—. *Siegfried's Journey*. Faber and Faber. 1945.

—. *Collected Poems, 1908–1956*. Faber and Faber. 1961. (Text used for poems).

SCOTT, Ralph. *A Soldier's Diary*. Collins. 1923.

SEEGER, Alan. *Letters and Diary of Alan Seeger*. Constable and Co. 1917.

—. *Poems*. Constable and Co. 1917.

SITWELL, Edith (ed.). *Wheels*. vols. 1–4. Oxford. 1916–1919. vol. 5 1920.

SITWELL, Osbert (later Sir). *Argonaut and Juggernaut*. Chatto and Windus. 1919.

—. *Left Hand, Right Hand!* 5 vols. Macmillan. 1946–50.

—. *Noble Essences*. (Vol. 5 of *Left Hand, Right Hand!*) Macmillan. 1950.

Soldier Poets. Erskine MacDonald. Trench Edition. 1916.

SORLEY, Charles Hamilton. *Marlborough and Other Poems*. C.U.P. Cambridge. 1916. (Text used for poems).

—. *The Letters of Charles Sorley*. C.U.P. Cambridge. 1919. (Text used for letters).

—. *The Poems and Selected Letters*. Ed. Hilda D. Spear. Blackness Press. Dundee. 1978.

THOMAS, Edward. *Collected Poems*. Faber and Faber. 1965. (Text used).

T[homas], H[elen]. *As It Was*. Faber and Faber. 1926.

TOMLINSON, H. M. *Waiting for Daylight*. Cassell. 1922.

—. *All Our Yesterdays*. Heinemann. 1930.

WEST, Arthur Graeme. *The Diary of a Dead Officer*. Allen and Unwin. nd. [1918].

The Wipers Times. A Facsimile Reprint of the Trench Magazines. Herbert Jenkins. 1918.

YEATS, W. B. *Collected Poems*. Macmillan. 1933. 2nd enlarged edition, 1950. (Text used).

—. *The Variorum Edition of the Poems of W. B. Yeats*. Ed. Peter Allt and R. K. Alspach. Macmillan. New York. 1957.

C. Secondary Sources

ALLEN, Clifford. *A Textbook of Psycho-Sexual Disorders*. O.U.P. 1962.

BATCHELOR, Ivor R. C. *Revision of Henderson and Gillespie's Text-book of Psychiatry*. O.U.P. 1969.

BERGONZI, Bernard. *Heroes' Twilight*. Constable. 1965.

BLUNDEN, Edmund. *Leigh Hunt*. Cobden-Sanderson. 1930.

—. *War Poets, 1914–1918*. British Council Pamphlet No. 100. 1958.

BOWRA, C. M. *Poetry of the First World War*. O.U.P. 1961.

BURNS, Robert. *Poems and Songs*. Ed. J. Kinsley. (rev. ed. Everyman's Library. 1959.)

COHEN, Joseph. 'Wilfred Owen's Greater Love'. *Tulane Studies in English*. VI. New Orleans. 1956.

—. 'Owen Agonistes'. *English Literature in Transition*, VIII. 5. 1965.

—. *Journey to the Trenches*. Robson Books. 1975.

COOKE, William. *Edward Thomas: A Critical Biography*. Faber and Faber. 1970.

CREWE, The Most Hon. the Marquess of. *War and English Poetry*. English Association Pamphlet No. 38. 1917.

CRUTTWELL, C. R. M. F. *A History of the Great War, 1914–1918*. Clarendon Press. Oxford. 1934.

CULPIN, Millais. *Psychoneuroses of War and Peace*. C.U.P. Cambridge 1920.

FALLS, Cyril. *War Books. A Critical Guide*. Peter Davies. 1930.

FARJEON, Eleanor. *Edward Thomas, The Last Four Years*. O.U.P. 1958.

FORSTER, E. M. *Abinger Harvest*. 1936. Penguin Books. 1967.

FOULKES, C. H. *'Gas!'* Blackwood and Sons. Edinburgh. 1934.

FUSSELL, Paul. *The Great War and Moden Memory*. O.U.P. 1975.

GREY, Viscount Edward of Fallodon. *Twenty-Five Years, 1892–1916*. 2 vols. Hodder and Stoughton. 1925.

HART, Liddell. *The War in Outline, 1914–1918*. Faber and Faber. 1936.

HASSALL, Christopher. *Rupert Brooke*. Faber and Faber. 1964.

HOPKINS, Gerard Manley. *A Selection of his Poems and Prose*. Ed. W. H. Gardner. Penguin Books. 1953.

HOULIHAN, Michael. *World War I: Trench Warfare*. Ward Lock. 1974.

HURST, Sir Arthur. *Medical Diseases of War*. (new ed.) Edward Arnold. 1940.

JOHNSTON, J. H. *English Poetry of the First World War*. O.U.P. 1964.

KIRKHAM, Michael. *The Poetry of Robert Graves*. Athlone Press. 1969.

KLEIN, Holger (ed.). *The First World War in Fiction: A Collection of Critical Essays*. Macmillan. 1976.

LEWIS, C. S. *Surprised By Joy*. Geoffrey Bles. 1955. Fontana edition, 1959.

LIDDIARD, Jean. *Isaac Rosenberg: The Half-Used Life*. Gollancz. 1975.

MASTERMAN, C. F. G. *The Condition of England*. Methuen. 1909. New edition, 1960.

MIZENER, Arthur. *The Far Side of Paradise*. Eyre and Spottiswoode. 1951.

MORAN, Lord Charles. *The Anatomy of Courage*. Constable. 1945.

OWEN, Frank. *Tempestuous Journey*. Hutchinson. 1954.

OWEN, Harold. *Journey From Obscurity*. 3 vols. O.U.P. 1963–1965.

—. *Aftermath*. O.U.P. 1970.

RIVERS, W. H. R. *Instinct and the Unconscious*. C.U.P. Cambridge. 1920. 2nd ed. with Appendices on War Neuroses. C.U.P. 1922.

ROSS, Robert H. *The Georgian Revolt*. Faber and Faber. 1967.

RUSSELL, Bertrand. *Portraits From Memory*. Allen and Unwin. 1956.

SILKIN, Jon. *Out of Battle*. O.U.P. 1972.

STALLWORTHY, Jon. *Wilfred Owen: A Biography*. O.U.P. 1974.

TAYLOR, A. J. P. *The First World War*. 1963. Penguin Books. 1966.

THORPE, Michael. *Siegfried Sassoon*. O.U.P. Leiden and London. 1966.

WELLAND, D. S. R. *Wilfred Owen*. Chatto and Windus. 1960.

WILLEY, Basil. *Spots of Time*. Chatto and Windus. 1965.

WILSON, Jean. *Isaac Rosenberg, Poet and Painter*. Cecil Woolf. 1975.

WORDSWORTH, William. *Collected Poems*. Ed. J. O. Hayden. 2 vols. Penguin Books. 1977.

YEATS, W. B. *The Letters of W. B. Yeats.* Ed. Allan Wade. Hart-Davis. 1954.

YEATS, W. B. (ed.). *The Oxford Book of Modern Verse.* Clarendon Press, Oxford. 1935.

·INDEX·

⋙━◈━⋙━◈━⋙━◈━⋙

157

158